THE
ASHEVILLE CONNECTION

THE
ASHEVILLE
CONNECTION

The Making of a Conservative

JOSEPH SCOTCHIE

Produced in the Republic of South Carolina by

SHOTWELL PUBLISHING LLC
Post Office Box 2592
Columbia, So. Carolina 29202
www.ShotwellPublishing.com

Cover Image: Adapted image from postcard owned by the publisher.

ISBN   978-1-947660-88-5

FIRST EDITION

10 9 8 7 6 5 4 3 2

THE ASHEVILLE CONNECTION

Is nostalgia for the Nineteen Sixties a little insane? Is that same sentiment for the Seventies more of the same? Maybe so, but in this memoir, Joseph Scotchie looks at the two Americas that existed in those times: Stable family life and a solid economy on one end, domestic and foreign strife on the other. In the early Sixties, a man could still support a growing family on a single paycheck, while in Baby Boom America no one talked of the coming death of the West. Scotchie takes the reader through events and experiences in two different, but representative American cities: Asheville, North Carolina and Youngstown, Ohio. Along the way, there are sketches of historical figures from that age: John F. Kennedy, Lyndon Johnson, Robert F. Kennedy, George Wallace, and Sam Ervin. A defense of the conservative Southern tradition and a volume that is, in part, a narrative, a reminiscence, a tribute, an essay and a polemic, *The Asheville Connection* presents a contrary view of American life during its days of burning.

AUTHOR'S NOTE

The events in this volume took place as the author remembered them. Names of certain institutions and individuals have been changed.

PERMISSIONS

Lyrics from "Song of the South" courtesy of The Walt Disney Co.

Lyrics from "Goodnight Saigon" courtesy of Universal Publishing Group

Lines from "The Strength of Fields" courtesy of Wesleyan University Press

TABLE OF CONTENTS

I.

STORK NATION

Nostalgia for the Sixties is insanity. The world had never seen anything like it. The early Sixties was a reasonably tolerable time, even for a utopian nation like the United States. Every morning, while men went to work, their wives stood on street corners with other moms and their children, sending them off to school. There was peace and prosperity, rising incomes, Christmas bonuses, optimism for the future. By the late Sixties, it looked to be over: Millions of Americans could no longer walk the streets of their own cities, nor could they even dream of sending their children to many of those same public schools. And there was more. As the sociologist Robert Nisbet famously claimed: "It would be difficult to find a single decade in the history of Western culture when so much barbarism—so much calculated onslaught against culture and convention...and so much sheer degradation of both culture and the individual—passed into print, into music, into art, and on to the American stage as the decade of the 1960s."

And yet there were two Sixties. The Kumbaya, Peace Corps, New Frontier-style optimism of the early Sixties, disintegrating by the end of the decade into a failed war and burnt cities. There was *The Andy Griffith Show* and *Petticoat Junction* nation here; the *Bob and Ted and Carol and Alice* and *Midnight Cowboy* one there. Two Sixties, but one common denominator: jobs were everywhere. Europe and Asia were recovering from World War II, catching up to America and

1

yet, the postwar boom was still on. Moreover, it was One Paycheck America. Think about it. In 1960, only 19 percent of young mothers were in the workforce, the other 81 percent were at home with their children. It was Baby Boom America. Throughout the late Forties, into the Fifties and the Sixties, the most common cartoon in any American newspaper was that of a smiling, grateful stork delivering a bundle to an expectant household. Normal America, too. A man, at age 35, could, most likely, look back on his still-young life and see a wife, two, three or more children, a car or two and a vacation at the beach. One Paycheck America and kids galore. Not only that, 95 percent of all births in the early Sixties were to a mother and father in holy matrimony.

Was the pre-Vietnam America that idyllic? So it seemed. Its symbol was the opening scene of *The Andy Griffith Show*: Andy and Opie walking down to the fishing hole, whistling away, Opie's rock skipping through the water. Behind closed doors, there was trouble. As John Updike observed, maybe people were getting married at too young an age. Married with children by 25? Yes, but party time still beckoned, especially in Updike's adulterous suburbia. Up to 17 percent of marriages ended in divorce. Still, traditional values would prevail. If a marriage went south, Dad had the book thrown at him. He got to see the kids on weekends. Dad also paid a healthy alimony bill, too.

Meanwhile, the kids tumbled out. We used to play a game in North Asheville: What street had the most kids? Our pals on Murdock Avenue said they had 42 kids. The grade schoolers on Edgewood Avenue said 53. On Baird Lane, where we lived before buying a house off Kimberly, maybe three dozen. Not bad. Well, that road, with no more than 10 houses was our Little Eden. The only childless home belonged to an older woman, a widow who kept an immaculate flower garden in her front lawn and was exceedingly friendly to my siblings and all the other children. Baby Boom America meant, also, boyhood brawl boom America. Once, a bigger kid, Billy Woodward, jumped on me during a big pile-up of us youthful brawlers. I thought my collar bone was broken. (It wasn't.) Your servant bawled away. This kindly lady broke things up and guided me home. The bigger kid kept coming by our house, bringing one gift after another. Maybe *he* thought my collar bone was broken. My mom would answer the door, I'd amble over and brush the guy off. Not necessary. At that age, you were just glad to mix it up. There was no shame in losing. When winter ended, Baird Lane and Lakeshore Drive swarmed with youngsters. We walked left past the Lytle's house (five children) to Beaver Lake, a man-made body of water built in the booming Fifties. Twice, it froze over for ice skating. My memories of the lake are melancholy. Early Saturday morning was great for fishing. And sometimes, fishing gets your mind off of upsetting results. By 1963, like every other boy in America, I was caught up with Mickey Mantle and the New York Yankees. The Mick! You grew up in America and had Willie Mays and Mantle as heroes. Impossible to top that. That fall, we all anxiously awaited the Yankee-Dodger World Series. Problem was that Sandy Koufax, now at the top of his game, stood in the way. The Dodgers won the first three games and in game four, with Koufax throwing bullets, they jumped out to a 1-0 lead on a Frank Howard home run. I was certain the game would end that way. But Mantle, to my surprise, tomahawked a high Koufax fastball into the Chavez Ravine bleachers to tie the score. However, the Dodgers scored on a throwing error by Tony Kubek (first basemen Joe Pepitone lost the ball in a sea of white shirts or so the scribes said). It was now the late innings. Koufax remained unhittable. My father didn't want me to see the Yanks losing on television, so he dragged us all to the lake to fish. We brought along a transistor. A typical Sunday afternoon crowd trolled the waters. Poor Mel Allen, the voice of the Yankees during those endless years of glory, couldn't take the humiliation—his mighty Yankees actually being swept in a World Series!—and so, he broke down on the air, weeping. His radio partner tried to calm him down. "C'mon, Mel. It's not that bad. It'll be alright." I fiddled with the bait, trying to understand a grown man crying. (His partner was right. Not that bad. Thirteen years later, in 1976, the Yankees won the pennant on a Chris Chambliss ninth inning home run. Billy Martin wept tears of joy. So did the Scooter, Phil Rizzuto. And Allen, although retired, still called an occasional game from the booth, thanks to the generosity of George Steinbrenner.)

Idyllic? No, but let the good times roll. Folks put up a good front. Divorced? Cough up that alimony bill. Public schools were fine, too. Normalcy was taken for granted. A mother could drop her children off at the bus stop in the morning, do housework and not worry at all about their safety, the usual assortment of bullies aside. My parents were part of the trickle of northerners moving South during the postwar era. Jobs were everywhere, as my mother once explained to me. Plus, my father was a graduate of Case Tech in Cleveland, which, as we learned, was considered the fourth best engineering school in the entire country. My father tried engineering in Roanoke, Cleveland, and Los Angeles before giving it a try in Asheville. I loved life in SoCal. Whiffle balls and butterfly hunts, a posse of us marching to a nearby grove to see what we could catch. There were swimming pools and my younger brother in diapers, walking happily in the front yard. A top star for the Dodgers was an outfielder named Wally Moon. "He hit the ball over the wall and he hit the ball over the moon," as my pals explained. It ended so quickly. Only one year in L.A., at the height of the aerospace boom. I remember, briefly, the plane ride east, the airborne ship making a turn over the Pacific, the blue ocean below us before turning towards the mountains. My mother later told me the plan: They'd stay for a year, then move on to an even better paying job than Northrup. But the mountains captured them. No sight is more beautiful than the Smokies, gold with leaves, each October. There was humor involved, also. Decades later, when my family celebrated my father's 70th birthday, he recalled, "I moved to Asheville and I...became...a Yankee!" (Midwesterners, especially those from Ellis Island stock, don't think that way, the term being confined to the Northeast and New England.) Life in Asheville was congenial. My folks became friends with other young couples from the St. Eugene's society. They, too, had large families. Why not? Catholic bishops had instructed married couples to have at least seven children. We fell one short, but my parents found plenty of company: The Keifer's (New York, five children), the Kane's (Philadelphia, six), the Rogers' (North Carolina, five), the Coughlin's (Chicago, five), the Haggerty's (Detroit, six) and the Hayes' (also North Carolina, five). All that business about a husband, a wife with two children and a dog was alien to me. People didn't have just *two* children. It was Brady Bunch America, a *With Six You Get Eggroll* land.

We were Catholic in the pre-Vatican II world, a conscience, but not a whiny minority in the Protestant, but tolerant Southland. (In the 1928 election, New York Irish Catholic Al Smith, the Democratic Party's nominee lost his home state of New York to Herbert Hoover, but carried such dry states as North Carolina, South Carolina, Georgia, Alabama, and Mississippi. In 1960, the centrist Irish Catholic John F. Kennedy managed to carry most of the Democratic Solid South). We'd discuss the new dispensation: Catholics and Protestants, the world of Baptists, Methodists, Presbyterians, Episcopalians. All struggled with the coming onslaught of modernity: The pill, movie ratings, school prayer out, no fault divorce in, with many unseen battles to come. Who's like us? we'd wonder aloud, before settling on the Episcopalians. They had priests. They received communion. One thing that wasn't debatable was religion itself. It was everywhere. A television variety program featured a comedian named Arthur Smith turned serious. He'd walk onto the stage, turn to the camera and announce, "This is the day the Lord hath made, let us rejoice and be glad." At McCormick Field, where the minor league Asheville Tourists played, a green billboard in the left field foul ground area shouted out, *SEE YOU IN CHURCH ON SUNDAY!* I never understood why it was there. This, after all, is Western North Carolina. *Everyone* goes to church on Sunday. We Catholics did. And I sure know Protestants did, also. Folks dressed in their Sunday best: Men in suits and ties, ladies in dresses, hats, white gloves and veils. My father gave me a quarter every Sunday morning just to shine his shoes. After services, folks packed into local restaurants for Sunday breakfast. Debates over religion raged on. Who were the true believers? Who were the slackers? What denominations were best suited to fight the modern world and its heresies?

In Asheville, I had fleeting memories of John F. Kennedy. My family members adored him. Why not? In 1960, he mopped the floor with 80 percent of the Catholic vote nationwide. Once, we all watched a television documentary on that same election. Richard

Nixon was shown in a good light, everyone cheering loudly at his stump speech, while Kennedy's talk was poorly received. I'd sit in the back of the car while an excerpt of a Kennedy speech filled the airwaves. All those big words, what do they mean? Guess I'll have to grow older before I can learn them. The local daily once carried a photo of Kennedy emerging from the ocean water onto the beach, surrounded by a bevy of beauties as if he were a movie star. The Bay of Pigs, the Berlin Wall, the summits with Nikita Khruschev were alien to me. I didn't know the world was set to blow over the Cuban Missile Crisis. My folks wisely kept such hysteria away from their children. My parents admired Kennedy. They, too, were at home in the Democratic Solid South. In fact, my father tooled around Asheville with a Kennedy for President sticker on our Carolina blue station wagon. It stayed there for the duration of the Kennedy presidency—-and years afterward, too.

The late November day was mild, an Indian summer in bloom. It was also a Friday. The school week was ending. As the final bell approached, the grade one room was quiet, content. Then a terrible, crackling sound shattered the calm. It came from the intercom in front of the class. One of the eighth grade students gave us the news: President Kennedy had been shot and was wounded. That was all. I didn't know that he was in Dallas. Instead, I pictured Kennedy in the front yard of the White House, ducking from the bullets behind the big trees. The school day ended. I trudged home alone, down Culvern, right to Beaverdam, across busy Merrimon, up that steep, steep hill next to the A & P, onto Lakeshore, around Beaver Lake, up another hill, right onto Baird Lane, into the house and there it was: My mother crying, sitting on the living room couch, inconsolable. A St. Eugene's neighbor, Mrs. Harbour was patting her on the back, smiling bravely and saying: "Oh, Connie, it's all right, it's all right. It will be all right." That did it. The lady was smiling while my mother wept. (Mrs. Harbour, to be fair, was concealing her own pain. She knew my mother would be distraught and so, she rushed over to our house.)

It had to be Mrs. Harbour. She was the only Republican in North Asheville. That's how Democratic North Carolina was in the early Sixties. If someone was a Republican, their name wasn't just Mrs. Harbour; no, it was "Mrs. Harbour, the Republican." I knew instantly that Kennedy was dead. Okay, the "where were you when you heard the news" story. It matters. Loss of innocence America still defines the day. And how! Only consider the electronic moment. Was it not the most symbolic event ever? CBS was the Tiffany of the networks, easily outpacing its two competitors. On that day, at that time, the network was airing a soap opera. At one moment, there is a housewife contentedly dusting off a shelf in free, happy, prosperous, at-peace, one-paycheck Baby Boom America. The next instant, the shocking news: The nation's dashing young prince—certain to be re-elected in 1964—had been assassinated by a miserable malcontent looking for fame.

It was a long weekend, a TV weekend. A *New York Times* article would proclaim those three days to be that medium's coming out. Television, not newspapers, was where the action was. We, too, were glued to the black and white images: Charles DeGaulle walking tall down Pennsylvania Avenue in full uniform; Halie Selassie, also in military gear, following the casket; Bobby Kennedy escorting the young widow, her face covered with a black veil; John-John's legendary tribute to his dead father; the long lines of mourners, suits and ties, dresses and high heels, all numbly walking past the flag-draped coffin. The ticker announced that Lee Harvey Oswald had been shot. A few hours later, the ticker added that Oswald was dead. "My God," my father blurted out. Why? I thought. The s.o.b. had it coming. And who can forget that Sunday? Pete Rozelle, the National Football League's young commissioner, made the call to go ahead with the full slate of games, some of which would be televised nationally. (It was a decision he later regretted.) Things were getting too surreal. At one instance, there was the file of people moving past the casket, a reality that now upset me greatly. Here was the young president, so alive at one moment, now in a casket. Out! Out! How can one get out? One couldn't, couldn't! Flick the channel and there was a football team racing downfield after the opening kickoff. "My

God," my mother complained. "How can they *do* such a thing?" My father stood there, silent. It was all true. How could anyone go running down a field on a weekend like that?

Loss of innocence? You bet—and then some. Years later, the witty columnist Joe Sobran claimed that the nation made a terrifying left turn after Kennedy's death. Kennedy a liberal? Not by today's standards. The man, after all, appointed a pro-life Western state Democrat, Byron "Whizzer" White to the Supreme Court. A conservative, as Ira Stoll has maintained? Not especially. Tax cuts, yes; spending reductions, no. Still, the country was flush with dough. There was immigration, where Kennedy had a visceral dislike for the National Origins Quota Act. That 1924 immigration cut-off bill was a reaction to the Ellis Island America that Kennedy sprang from. The resentful young president had wanted to change it, by eliminating the British Isles-only quota for immigration from anywhere in the world. Such legislation went nowhere on his watch, the U.S. Congress still containing a large bloc of conservative Southern Democrats. With the failure of the Bay of Pigs and the inability to overthrow Castro, the New Frontiersmen turned their sites to South Vietnam, under siege from a communist, nationalist movement from the North, a nation earlier given security assurances from the Eisenhower Administration. In 1983, Arthur Schlesinger, Jr. claimed that JFK, if re-elected, would not have committed more U.S. troops to Vietnam. Was it true? Loss of innocence? Yes, but who knew it at the time? In early 1964, The Beatles came to America, filling a void left by JFK's death. That same year, Lyndon Johnson won a landslide election to the White House. The U.S. economy grew by an incredible 25 percent. "These are the most hopeful times since Christ was born in Bethlehem," the vainglorious Johnson proclaimed after his big win. Alas, Sobran would be proved correct. Early Sixties? Kumbaya and Peace Corps. Late Sixties? The Vietnam morass and once-vital cities in flames. The nation did take that hard turn left and the Sixties would turn out badly, very badly indeed.

II.

WHEN DOWNTOWN WAS THE WORLD

"What a town this is!" my father blurted out one spring evening as we sped through Valley Street on the way to McCormick Field for a Double-A game. "In Youngstown you have to drive *all* the way to Cleveland for a game. Here, you just have to get in the car and boom," he slapped the wheel with his hand, "you're at the ballpark."

Truth is, the Asheville Tourists, then a Pittsburgh Pirates affiliate, were a terrific team all throughout the Sixties. Willie Stargell, Bob Robertson, Dock Ellis and Gene Alley all made it to The Big Show. The top heroes were such local legends as Elmo Plaskett and Duncan Campbell, both of whom the fans loved. My father took great joy in family outings. Engineering, his profession, was a high stress job. And so, Sundays were often spent at Craggy Gardens on the parkway, NASCAR races on the radio as my father navigated his own sharp turns. He liked going to ballgames with the children the best. After the Pirates left Asheville, there came the Cincinnati Reds as the Tourists' new affiliate. That meant the skipper Sparky Anderson, plus Dave Concepcion, the immortal Bernie Carbo, Darrell Chaney, and Wayne Simpson, all of whom played the 1968 season in Asheville and then, just two years later, in the 1970 World Series. The Redleg years also included Kurt Bevacqua, who later played in the 1984 World Series for the San Diego Padres. One night, with the score tied in extra innings, Bevacqua led off with a solid single to left field. Not content to start off a possible game-winning inning with a hit, Bevacqua tried to turn it into a double and was thrown out by a country mile. "Dum-dum, what a dum-dum," was all my father could say. He went on and on. The fact that both Bevacqua and my father had an Eastern European ancestry might have had something to do with it. He made us look bad. From that moment on, the name was Kurt "Dum Dum" Bevacqua, as if the play was the only thing he ever did on a baseball diamond.

What a town. You bet! Starting off as Morristown in 1793, the village, as with many similar municipalities in Western North Carolina was later renamed for a Revolutionary War hero, in this case, Samuel Ashe, an Albemarle native who helped to draft the state's new constitution following North Carolina's break from the British crown, while also serving a term as governor once independence was established. The South, as Weaverville's favorite son, Richard M. Weaver once observed, was the place that history happened to. And so too with Asheville. With the arrival of the Vance clan, the town began to make its mark. With that family, namely the meteoric career of Zebulon Vance, North Carolina had its own political dynasty. Originally from the western counties, members of the Vance family served in both the Revolutionary War and the War of 1812. Dr. Robert Vance was a U.S. Congressman. Zeb's maternal grandfather, Zebulon Baird, was a state legislator. As a youngster growing up in the Montford section, Zeb Vance witnessed John C. Calhoun's visit to town. That inspired the young man to enter a career in politics. Vance rose quickly through the ranks: Chapel Hill Law School, Buncombe County Democratic Party politics and election to the U.S. House of Representatives at age 28 in 1860, right time for the Secession Summer of 1861. Vance, like most Tar Heels, said "no" to secession, but also "no" to war. Fort Sumter settled the issue. No summer soldier, Vance quickly assembled a regiment and marched north, to the Virginia theatre. When North Carolina's governor, Joseph Ellis, died in 1863, the 31-year-old Vance was the consensus choice, from Murphy to Manteo, to take the job. The War Between The States represents Asheville's moment in history. By 1865, this town of 1,000 inhabitants had the state's governor (Vance), its attorney general (Augustus Merrimon) and the popular president of the University of North Carolina (David Swain). The town housed an important munitions dump. The Battle of Asheville, a skirmish that took place both before and after Appomattox, was a victory for a local Confederate militia (word passed slowly in those days).

After the war, both Merrimon and Vance maintained their prominence. Vance succeeded Merrimon as one of the state's U.S. senators, with the irrepressible Zeb now serving as the voice of calm and reason as the leader of that body's now-embattled Southern states delegation. The names from the war ring out: Merrimon Avenue, the Vance monument, Coxe Avenue, McDowell Street, Clingman's Dome, all named for Confederate pols, veterans and in the case of Thomas Clingman, a U.S. senator who, unlike Vance, did support secession immediately following the election of Abraham Lincoln in 1860. But who remembers these gents? The roadside plaque for David Swain stands on Merrimon Avenue, sandwiched in between traffic lights, shopping centers, gas stations and nightclubs. The great man seems lonely in such a place.

The next big moment came in 1880 with the construction of a railroad depot. Asheville graduated from small town to a medium-sized city. The Twenties' boom was on the horizon, but for now, the next great figure in the town of Zeb Vance and Thomas Wolfe was George Pack, the Ohio native and legendary philanthropist. Other movers and shakers were George Vanderbilt and Lloyd Grove, the latter a developer also from the Midwest. Vanderbilt, heir to a famous New York family, built his mansion in Biltmore Forest, but he died young. His wife carried on, content with charitable work, such as the Baker YHI. Of Pack and Grove, the former was far more beloved by the natives. Why? Well, Pack's wife had become ill with a serious throat ailment. He moved to Asheville for the cure and the city's mountain climate worked its magic. Mrs. Pack recovered and her husband immediately made Asheville the family home. He delivered monies for the library and for the completion of the Vance monument on what would eventually be Pack Square. Grove was a builder: Residential neighborhoods, a downtown arcade, an attractive resort hotel. Grove saw real estate and money. Pack, like

Vanderbilt, wanted to uplift the cultural spirits of the city. Well, the Pack Library is where the young Tom Wolfe spent his childhood devouring volume after volume. That reaped some handsome dividends and this author fondly remembers that stone building and musty shelves before its demise in the late Seventies.

Grove, more than the gentle Pack, was the city's prophet of the Roaring Twenties. Who can forget that famous photo of a wary Grove with the three greats all vacationing in Asheville? A relaxed and tanned Henry Ford, a plump, contented Thomas Edison, and an amused Henry Firestone. Mass production of automobiles, motion pictures, electric lighting, long distance phone calls, the tires to run those machines on. The men who made a century! No, the men who created the world for billions upon billions yet born. The boom was on. Why bother with hot, muggy Florida when you can have Asheville's cool, green mountains? In quick order came the City and County buildings, a spanking new high school, the Jackson Building, all in the handsome Art Deco style that would become the city's architectural trademark.

In addition to the mansion, Vanderbilt's other contribution was a fine, brick hotel on the edge of downtown. Two Asheville's came together: The ballroom dancing on Saturday nights from the hotel and the honky tonks on Lexington. Either way, the Twenties' boom was in full motion. Real estate speculation fueled the rush. No one imagined that it could end. As such, the 1929 Crash devastated Asheville. The city's banks lost more money than their counterparts in such larger municipalities as Charlotte, Raleigh, Greensboro, and Winston-Salem. When the banks closed, crowds thronged to the locked doors. Life savings vanished. The mayor committed suicide. "A wounded bear" is how Mitzi Tessier described Asheville in her pictorial history of the city. It was old-fashioned thrift rather than New Deal programs that got the city out of its rut. The somber Curtis Bynum took over city finances. No one questioned his belt-tightening as the recovery slowly took shape. Still, the debt from the crash wasn't paid off entirely until 1975.

After the Depression came World War II, a conflict whose American involvement was opposed by Robert Reynolds, "Buncombe Bob," the colorful anti-prohibition U.S. senator from Asheville, the last man from the mountain town to win a statewide office. Reynolds, an opponent of mass immigration, but a supporter of Federal funds for the Blue Ridge Parkway, correctly predicted that Joe Stalin would be the eventual political winner of the war. Needless to say, it didn't work. The war remains a mythic period in American history. For his part, Reynolds opted out of a 1944 re-election campaign that he could not have won. America, too, was a huge winner from the war. With the economies of Europe and Asia decimated, the U.S. ruled, militarily and financially, like no nation in world history. The world, indeed, was now American. And at home, the boom picked up again in the Fifties. Once again, downtown was the world, in this pre-mall America, a nation that I prefer very much to the one that replaced it. The city's future jumbo mall was still a driving range in East Asheville. The Sixties downtown was a place where the Plaza Theater and its Saturday afternoon Disney movies for grade schoolers stood across the street from pool halls with winos and bums and hustlers.

Best of all, not much had changed over the decades. The downtown of Charlie Justice, the future All-American football great, darting through shoppers on a busy Patton Avenue during the Christmas season rush with his buddies all pretending they were footballers, was still there. The same was true for my pals and me in the still innocent Sixties: The cigar store next to the pool hall with newspapers and magazines; the Imperial Theater on College Street with the "world's greatest newspaper stand" (I believed it!) doing business in front of it; Kress's with cheeseburgers and milk shakes; the inevitable Woolworth's where you could buy all the Christmas gifts for folks and siblings in one afternoon; Pritchard Park, where a lone Baptist preacher held court from the early morning hours onward. The Big Three department stores—Belk's, J.C. Penny, Bon Marche—stayed put for now, my mother dragging me to them one Saturday morning. One shirt, pants, pairs of shoes after another being tried on as the ladies had a few laughs over my sour behavior, the Man's Store, the music stores, the bike shop on the corner of Patton and Coxe (this was my father's

13

place, on Saturday mornings, we walked into this little dugout, full of grease and oil and bicycle chains and frames, my father was a born mechanic), the blue Schwinn ruled the kids' streets. Up on Pack Square was the library bearing that same name. Here, I got a whiff of the future, reading a book on a sportswriter's life in New York. What fun! Ballgames in the summer, banquets in the winter months. There was Saroyan's *Places Where I've Done Time*, Salinger's *The Catcher In The Rye* and Bellow's *Henderson The Rain King*. The book reading bug came later on, but the library had its old-fashioned charms. The narrow entrance was cozy, the Thomas Wolfe collection on the second floor was extensive. In time, I went from a gym rat to a library creature. Plus, it was a fine place to meet girls (those members of the opposite who think the way you do).

When did downtown come alive? Not so much on business weekdays as on Saturday mornings. There was the Farmer's Market, jammed to capacity with shoppers. It was a place where country folk came to town, some of them still hungover. One morning, my father drove us by the crowded sidewalks on Patton Avenue. A red-faced young man and his girl were arguing, screaming at each other; fists (from the girl) were flying. "Don't look! Don't look!" my father shouted at us, grabbing us away from the window. My parents, products of blue collar Ohio—a turf as rowdy as it gets— were nonetheless wary of these country people and their ways. They thought it was a bad influence on the middle class manners they had fashioned for us. "Don't say 'ain't!'" my mother would yell whenever that word came from our mouths. "Don't *say* that word!" A cuss word was worse. "If you talk that way again, I'll wash your mouth out with soap!" my mother also warned. Being kids, we played with fire. Next thing you know, I'm under the bathroom sink, my mouth full of that mixture of hot water and a bar of soap being run across my mouth like a lumberjack sawing a big oak tree. Happened once. Happened twice. That was it. Got the message. It wasn't that bad, but my mother did not like "ain't" at all. Other than any given Saturday, the biggest event was the annual Christmas parade. There were others. In 1962, there was a big parade downtown for Maria Beale Fletcher, the Asheville girl who had just been crowned Miss

America. For years, a stunning portrait of this classy woman hung in the dining room of the Biltmore Dairy House. The next year, 1963, saw a big bash for Charlie Justice, one celebrating his election to the College Football Hall of Fame.

The highlight of the annual parade was the South French Board marching band. Floats and bands and organizations filed by, but as the parade neared its end, an excited buzz zipped its way through the crowds. "They're coming! They're coming!" People shuffled their feet in anticipation. The high-stepping band did not disappoint. Band leaders, majorettes, instrument-playing band members brought down the house. Yes, this was the downtown of the Old Kentucky Home, the Thomas Wolfe residence coming into its own as a National Historic Landmark as Asheville slowly made its peace with the world famous novelist, the real bitterness towards Wolfe's autobiographical 1929 classic, *Look Homeward, Angel* wearing away as many of the residents caricatured by the unsuspecting young novelist were on passing on (Wolfe, in his 1937 return to Asheville, countered that bitterness with sincere apologies, plus students at Lee Edwards High School were thrilled to meet the man). It was also the downtown under happy Greek rule; that is, the Greek-American owned eateries. My pal Dean Peterson's family had a restaurant on the square. Elsewhere, Two Brothers and Three Brothers and Four Brothers restaurants at least to the mind, proliferated.

This was Safe America. My folks and those of my friends allowed us to wander the streets by ourselves. One Saturday, my pal Marky Rollins was on the loose for a single, "I've Just Got To Get A Message To You" by the Bee Gees. In and out of music stores we went, searching down that little 45. Marky was in a hurry. We left North Asheville early. I didn't have time to slick down my hair, leaving me self-conscience about the Alfalfa-style cowlick springing up in the back of my head. After the fifth or sixth store, some clerk made the inevitable crack about my hair standing up on its end. Everyone laughed, but at least the lance was boiled. It wasn't that bad. After about the tenth store, Marky snagged the little black round single. (It was the start of a promising career. Marky loved communications. He had a LP record on the history of baseball that played the famous

Russ Hodges broadcast of the legendary 1951 Bobby Thomson home run that won the pennant that year for the New York Giants over the Brooklyn Dodgers. ("The Giants win the pennant! The Giants win the pennant! They're going crazy! I don't believe it! The Giants win the pennant!" There was also the 1948 recording of Babe Ruth's sad farewell address at Yankee Stadium, in which the Babe, stricken with cancer, hailed the youth of America for their devotion to the great game (Babe, to the end, loved children.)) Marky played those recordings over and over again just like Rudy Ruettiger playing the Knute Rockne pep talks at the beginning of *Rudy*. Before you knew it, Marky was on AM radio in town, putting out pretty good one liners before spinning a top pop song. He went on to even greater heights in the Midwest, scoring a top job at a station in Indianapolis.

That was our downtown. It represented some of the terrain, but not all of it. In the early Eighties, I read Fred Chappell's succinct novel of the Sixties' downtown, *The Gaudy Place*. Years later, when I read it again, that world came back to me on the novel's final pages: All the joints and their colorful names: The Tip Top, Smokey the Bar, the Flamingo Inn, and others so raunchy they didn't even have a storefront sign. That wasn't my world. I'd stare into the pool halls and honky tonks, at the old salts and painted ladies, Hank Senior and Patsy Cline on the box. I wouldn't dream of stepping in, even when I was of age. No place for a boy whose folks worked diligently for their middle-class status. Still, downtown was the world. Honky tonk and G-rated culture sat side-by-side. Movie houses and department stores were there; so, too, was theater. Here was another North Asheville connection. A youngster named Hal James had a gift for theater productions. As a high school student, he began doing theater in his garage and front lawn, ones that expanded to the Tanglewood Theater, first in a location off Merrimon Avenue, then downtown to sold out productions at various venues. The auditions were held in the grand ballroom of The Vanderbilt Hotel. My father signed me up for a *Babes In Toyland* tryout. These auditions were on a fall afternoon. The lobby television, as I sauntered by, blared out, "and Bill Russell pulled down 27 rebounds in the Celtic win," while the thespians performed. (I was stuck near the end.) My turn came and I'm on a stage, singing "Zippity-Doo-Dah" from *Song Of The South*. The piano player banged on, giving me great confidence as I plunged forward.

Mr. Bluebird's on my shoulder

It's the truth, it's factual

Everything is satisfactual

A singer? Not a chance! Still, I could hit the "zippity" note. In the front row, I noticed a heavy-set, red-faced man watching and tapping along. That's right, get 'em tapping. More confidence for me. Even on stage, I realized how much Southerners appreciated even this small tribute to their heritage. The song was a good choice. The natives liked it if you said/sang/wrote something nice about the always-beleaguered Southland. And such gestures were still possible in the early Sixties. No singer, indeed! Still, I snagged a tin soldier part. At the end of the play, we'd march onstage and tie a rope around the waist of the villain. Rehearsals were at an old hall off Biltmore Avenue, across from the foreboding Fine Arts Theater (a dirty movie joint that scared young minds). The rehearsals were more fun than the performance. Would-be actors, actresses and hangers-on did their part to make the play a success. One of them, a red-haired teenager named Georgia aroused our pre-adolescent emotions. A red-haired girl, with her own dressing kit, her own locker, her own makeup box, too. A real pro! I thought. She had the dot on the cheek, Marilyn Monroe-style and pretended not to notice all the amateurs she was stuck with. This girl was going places. We stared, the same sensation that happened when the opening credits of *Petticoat Junction* rolled by, the inn proprietor's three daughters with their bloomers draped over the water tower, getting dry. Red hair, blue eye shadow, red lipstick, a figure and a saucy, Southern name. All of this was several years up the road.

Meanwhile, I was in a bigger jam. One night, my ride home had left without me, leaving me stranded on a pitch dark, empty weekday night on Biltmore Avenue, the Fine Arts Theater scarier than ever. I was nervous, but only briefly so. On the same avenue was a parked police car, with two young officers inside. I marched right over, told 'em of my dilemma and my address, 23 Baird Lane. I hopped in the back and the officers dutifully drove me home. At the doorstep, I proudly told my father about my adult-like decisiveness. My police car had turned around and tooled down Baird Lane. My father yelled out, "Hey, fellows!" but they didn't hear. The police were the good guys. (As the disillusioned Frank Serpico observed, "they know, they know.") Of course you went to them. How this would change. In time, the climate took a shocking turn. Police were now "pigs," guilty of unspeakable brutality. Indeed, by 1967, the finest, it sometimes seemed, had become human targets just about every time they stepped out of the house.

Not every adventure was so eventful. Most forays were solo and if not, thoroughly family filled. Our favorite was the S & W cafeteria, another Art Deco masterpiece. It was the most democratic place in town, a reminder of when folks would put in a day at the office, then retire to a downtown eatery. Businessmen and busboys, blue collar and professionals, the food was typical Southern fare: Fried chicken, biscuits, mashed potatoes and gravy, meat loaf, sweetened ice tea, plus coffee and pe-*cahn* (as opposed to pe-*can*) pie. The Lee Edwards cheerleaders sitting and laughing at an upstairs booth gave me another *Petticoat Junction* moment.

That was for dining out. For sports, there was the city YMCA, located in the Woodfin House on College Street. Here, on Saturdays, us St. Eugene's boys mixed it up with public school kids (on Sundays, we had it out with other Catholic schools). The basketball court had an overhead track, which played Bill Russell, slapping down many an outside shot from the far corners. Ever since 1956, when the UNC Tar Heels, an insane squad coached by the New York Irish Catholic Frank McGuire and a starting lineup of Lenny Rosenbluth, Tommy Kearns, Pete Brennan, Joe Quigg and Bob Cunningham upset Kansas and its freshman center, Wilt Chamberlain, North Carolina became a basketball state. Dean Smith's Tar Heels now ruled the roost, fending off Everett Case's N.C. State team and Vic Buba's Duke Blue Devils. Plus, my uncle Bob, the youngest of six boys, was a high school basketball star in the highly competitive Mahoning County, Ohio jungle of blue-collar high school students. He later played college ball, all of which impressed me greatly. We all played, but the Y also had a swimming pool, a modest affair, with small tile bleachers for tournaments. Don Schollander, losing in the 1968 Olympics to Don Rogers in the 100-meter butterfly moved me also. So, too, did another uncle, Irv, a native of Brooklyn who married my mother's younger sister and who was a lifeguard in *The Summer Of '42*-style New York at Rockaway Beach. That big man could swim, lapping the pool twice underwater. Swimming, even more than basketball, was the top Y sport. And it mattered, since the Asheville Y swim team featured the young Mary Montgomery, who soon became the city's first Olympiad, plus a multi-year winner of the North Carolina Female Amateur Athlete of the Year award. Mary's mother was the coach. Mrs. Montgomery worked us hard. The best my pals and myself could earn were a few medals as a relay team competing in meets in Spartanburg and Greenville. Mary impressed me more than Miss Georgia. Plus, she inspired the team to reach for greater heights. The grand old Y had a spacious lobby with numerous sofas. A big oak tree cast a shadow over the entire front lawn. History was made in these quarters. In 1861, following Fort Sumter, a somber meeting of John Woodfin, Zeb Vance and Augustus Merrimon discussed—-and supported—the state's secession from the Union, something it had wanted to avoid following the election of 1860.

"Godamm hilly street, godamm hilly town," muttered Arky, the young hero of *The Gaudy Place*. Yes, and down from the Woodfin House was the Farmer's Market, the most fun place in town for a proper, middle-class lad. Here were characters right out of William Faulkner and Flannery O'Connor: Gaunt men in black wool hats and overalls, plump women in old dresses; pickup trucks and old jalopies. The dusty lot gave way to the outdoor marketplace: Peas, carrots, corn, radishes, tomatoes: Hands dumping the barrels down, hands spreading the produce out, hands sorting out the ripe from the sour: Faster, faster, faster all the time. The clatter among the farmers, their wives, the customers: Faster and faster, too. Couldn't get enough of this place and these hectic, but satisfied people so far as it was from my middle-class world.

It was more than that. The market reminded me of my grandparents' farm in northeastern Ohio. Both of my grandfathers worked in the mills before starting their own businesses. But they both kept a connection to the past, growing those same vegetables in their backyards (My maternal grandfather had five acres of land in suburban Austintown. His garden turned a tidy profit.) These county folk weren't so far removed from that same past. After all, America, prior to World War II, was still a nation of small towns and rural areas, occasionally punctuated by large, but safe, cities. The family farm, circa 1940, was an ongoing thing. These farmers, too, probably worked in the mills outside of town, but they kept their own gardens in the backyard. This was the early Sixties. A middle-aged man or a senior grew up in that old Family Farm America that had survived the country's transformation to an urban-industrial society. These men and women lived there still. Every time I wandered alone downtown, I always made the pit stop at the Farmers Market, mostly to watch and hear: One, two, three times, then—-gone! Just like that, the market moved to more spacious quarters beyond West Asheville. I could understand the motive (without liking the move at all). These farmers lived outside of town, so did their customers. Once the East Asheville mall was built in the early Seventies, no one came to town on Saturdays. What for? Plus, the market needed larger quarters for their bounty. It was, after all, a prosperous endeavor. No one can subsist on sentiment. Often, I'd drive past the Farmer's Market exit sign on I-26. But I never pulled off the highway.

Why did my folks let me wander? Why did Marky's folks allow him to do the same? It was Safe America, Happy America. My folks liked the idea, I think, of living in a city where you were close to town, where everything you needed was downtown and where it was perfectly safe for grade school kids, alone or in a pack, to adventure all day on Saturday. Plus, we had that big, Catholic family. Seven, soon to be eight, under one roof. You can't be spoiled in such an arrangement. You learned early to fend for yourself. So, line 'em up again: The Plaza, pool halls, cigar shops, the Imperial, Kress's, Bon Marche, J.C. Penny's, Woolworth's, the library, the Farmer's Market, Old Kentucky Home, Pritchard Park, Gordon's Jewelry, Peterson's Grill on Pack Square. It all ended up at the big bus stop in front of the library. Forget Car 54. Merrimon-Midland, where are you? That's the bus that took me to Baird Lane. One by one, the buses would steam past: Merrimon-Beaverdam, Merrimon-Charlotte, Merrimon-Kimberly. The day grew longer. I was the only boy left at the stop. Dusk had settled in. Merrimon-Griffin, Merrimon-Pearson. Darker still. Yeah, I got scared (but police department headquarters were right down the block!). Finally, in full sight, Merrimon-Midland. Sigh. Ah. That's more like it. The bus ride was fine, also. The Sixties-style buses had plush, cushiony seats, fat and plump; you sunk right in and enjoyed the ride. The buses also had wires that you pulled as your stop approached. A grade schooler felt like the big boss man. Pull that wire—ding!, Mr. Bus Driver, you gotta pull right over and let the young master out. Did it once, did it twice, all as if I had something to prove. Trolley cars were gone, but the city buses were spacious and comfortable. The day, from morning to dusk, was an adventure. Everything was in its ordered place—-North, South, East and West Asheville, plus Church Street and Main Street back in the days before the mall when, to me, downtown was the world.

III.

The Sun Shines Bright

"Wherever the Catholic sun doth shine/there's always laughter and good red wine/at least I've always found it so/ Benedicamus Domino!"

So sang that great Belloc. Just as true in southern France as in southern U.S.A. The St. Eugene's families were close. Easy to see why. In the late Forties and Fifties, with America triumphant and supremely confident, couples married young. (By 1955, half of all women at age 20 were married.) They had children right away. So such couples liked to socialize. My folks and other St. Eugene's parents had dinner parties and bridge games. They played Mitch Miller records and went to retreats at St. John Vinnany Hall. When one couple got divorced, it was a shocker. It just can't happen. For Catholics, divorce was against the law. I mean against, as in no exceptions.

These gatherings were part of the times, that trickle of northerners who began moving South, first in the Twenties and then picking up again in the Fifties. The St. Eugene's school, a brick building with a ballfield and a rectory cottage across the street was constructed in that same decade. Masses were held in the auditorium. In 1969, a church with a tall steeple was built, down the street on Culvern. Church officials were delighted, comparing the event to the glory days of the Middle Ages. When we first moved to Asheville, we lived in a tidy little colony of cottages right next to the school. Shortest walk ever. Then, the little colony was obliterated to make room for a supermarket. No matter. We needed more real estate, anyway.

The school grounds, meanwhile, were always packed on weekends. Yes, we kept up with the Protestants, debating which ones were like us. But as with First Baptist Church or Grace Episcopal, the church, not necessarily the schools, were the center of social life. There was bingo, but also huge pot roast dishes: The women in the kitchen, while outside, the kids went wild with kickball and basketball in basketball-crazy Carolina. After Sunday mass, the men discussed UNC basketball. Chris Daniels, Timmy Randall and myself all hung out on a bench while the men mourned the big loss in the 1967 NCAA finals to UCLA. We didn't pay much attention. After all, Chris, Touchee (the great man's nickname) and myself all played the game. Every Saturday in the fall and winter, there was the YMCA league games against public schools. Every Sunday, we went up against Catholic school teams. That was a tough schedule. The public school kids were a formidable matchup against little Catholic schools. Games were played early Saturday morning at the foreboding Jerome Pressley High School gym, also alien turf for us. On Sundays, they were played at the spacious Asheville Catholic gym, a place packed with screaming crowds, many of them on your side. On Sunday after church, Chris, Timmy and myself recuperated from the Saturday battles and caught our breath for the next round that afternoon. Nothing tops male bonding and Chris, I am happy to say, made out the best of us, becoming a Catholic priest.

Years later, at my parish in Douglaston, Queens, I heard a young priest recall the days when Catholic school tuition was non-existent. Schools were free—just like public institutions. Was it so in Asheville? Maybe so. St. Eugene's was staffed, almost entirely, by nuns and priests. It only had one or two lay teachers. At St. Eugene's, pews were full on Sundays and weeknight masses, too. Collection money paid the bills. Easy to see why. Standing guard was Father Brown, the grand old man of St. Eugene's and his assistant, the studious Father Pharr. Everyone loved Father Brown. You couldn't imagine St. Eugene's without him. He was a crusty old priest right out of the

Spencer Tracy character in *Boys Town*. At report card time, he'd come around to all of the classes and hand out the document to each student. It was no fun. Father Brown would call your name, look at the marks and then give you a good dressing down if they weren't high enough. One boy, Peter Doyle, got such a tongue lashing that he broke down, sobbing. It was sad, but I was glad that Father Brown spent all of his anger on him. When it was my turn (my marks were always mediocre at best), the fire was gone. Otherwise, Father Brown was very much the Marcus Welby, M.D. of St. Eugene's. He'd use his backyard of the parish cottage as a mini-driving range, lifting one golf ball after another onto the ballfield below. He knew I was a huge sports fan. I once showed him a drawing of my two idols, Mickey Mantle and Willie Mays. He chuckled at the sincere, first grade effort at authenticity. He let me into the rectory living room to watch Game One of the 1963 World Series between the Yankees and the Dodgers. It was the first time I had ever viewed a color television set and the scenic beauty of the packed Yankee Stadium grandstands, all decked out in red, white, and blue World Series bunting was thrilling to me. That was enough. My mother wisely took me home before Sandy Koufax's fastballs and wicked curves shut down my beloved pinstrippers.

Father Brown was there for the duration, from the parishes' founding in the Fifties to the bleak post-Vat II days of the early Seventies. He was the granite, Mt. Rushmore-style face of St. Eugene's. In my later years there, some classmates tried to turn the student body against him. Can you believe the gall? By the seventh grade, we had a popular History teacher, a Mr. Lynch from Milwaukee, who was set to be married. We all liked him. Mr. Lynch was easy-going and knowledgeable as he guided us through antiquity, the glory of the Roman Empire, the Middle Ages, the Industrial Revolution and onward. He was a lay teacher, but nothing he taught was contrary to church doctrine. According to rumors, Mr. Lynch was co-habituating with his fiancé, a divorcee with children. Was it true? The word, apparently, got out to Father Brown. He told Mr. Lynch to stop living in such an arrangement. The teacher refused. And so, Father Brown dismissed him. Time had now moved from the early to late Sixties. Students tried to organize with cheers, rallies, and demonstrations. To hell with "the times," Father Brown was still the face of St. Eugene's.

The cause went nowhere. Plus, there were plenty of young teachers eager for work. I didn't go along with the rebels. Neither did the parents of any of the upset students. Mr. Lynch was a fine, dedicated teacher, but you just don't defy the church. Father Brown's associate, Father Pharr, was tall, bespectacled, solidly built and scholarly. One Saturday afternoon, while everyone else was wrapping up a long, happy day playing ball, you'd see Father Pharr walking quietly from the auditorium to the rectory. I know what he was doing: Memorizing the sermon for Sunday mass. It was serious business. Then there were the nuns. And how! Enough for each grade. It was the old Catholic Church: Irish nuns, Italian-American nuns from Ethnic America, later on, nuns from the Philippines. Sister Colleen, Sister Pauline and Sister Carmello, the latter an olive-skinned nun from Brooklyn who whizzed fast-pitched underhand fastballs right past our flailing swings. Sister Pauline was my favorite. She was our first grade teacher and who *doesn't* have a crush on a grade school marm? There was Sister Pauline, a native of the Emerald Island itself; Sister Pauline, who had us, one and all, believing in leprechauns; Sister Pauline, who needed her shoes tied. At attention! We'd drop to our knees like buck privates and furiously tie those laces, the black dress covering the black shoes. Nuns wore habits, the white "forehead" and everything else, including the cross and rosaries around the neck, in black. One Halloween, my father brought us over to the nun's rectory. We were too shy to talk, but plenty thrilled at being in their actual living quarters. Yes, we volunteered for those shoe-tying drills. The nuns enjoyed the company, sitting down together on the couch, all in a row. Wouldn't you know that Sister Pauline would leave after that year, assigned to another parish? After all this, reader, you can't be surprised that Chris and Tim and my other pals all served as altar boys. More serious business. The first mass we worked was nerve-racking, just like the first Little League or Y football or basketball game. We'd earnestly chant through those passages in our thick prayer books.

Sanctus, Sanctus, Sanctus,

Dominus Deus Sabaoth

Pieni sunt caeli et terra

Gloria tua

Hosanna in excelsis

Benedictus qui venit in nomine Domini

Hosanna in excelsis

We felt bad if we missed a cue, such as ringing the communion bell at the wrong time or failing to bring the water and wine and most important, the hosts to the altar when needed. Afterwards, in the altar boy locker, we'd feel down, as if we had just lost a big playoff game, until one of the church regulars, a matronly lady who could see we were glum would come by and cheer us up by saying what a great job we did. We all served from first through eighth grade. To this day, I bristle when someone makes a smart aleck remark about the breed:

"We're not exactly *altar* boys at this investment firm."

"We want players who can win. If we wanted to win with altar boys, we'd go to the church steps and pick up some."

"Well, I didn't behave like an *altar* boy in between marriages!"

No altar boy, eh? I'll give you an altar boy, one from that same era of the late Fifties and early Sixties. Try Rocky Versace, a subject in S. Cort Kirkwood's stemwinder, *Real Men*. Altar boy! Yes, Rocky, a native of Washington, D.C., was an altar boy at his local parish in Alexandria, Virginia. In the book, Rocky is shown assisting with communion, that big, golden spatula under the priest's fingers, ensuring that the host will not drop to the floor. Rocky, emulating his father, attended West Point, graduating in 1959. In 1961, he volunteered for service in Vietnam, where the Kennedy Administration was waging low-level war. Rocky served as an Army

Ranger. In 1963, he became a prisoner of war. No way could the Viet Cong break him. They tortured his legs, kept him in irons. He still clammed up. They put Rocky in re-education camps. Meanwhile, Rocky, now prematurely gray, made friends with local Vietnamese youth, who all loved the good-natured American prisoner. Why not? Rocky had faith. He knew, also, that his faith was being tested. There would be no stateside glory. Rocky, as he accepted, would meet his end in a North Vietnamese prison camp, but he never gave an inch. There were, as you shall see, Rocky Versace-types from Asheville, too. Being an altar boy at St. Eugene's was something you did, like playing the Big Three—football, basketball, and baseball. It went hand-in-hand with the Latin mass.

"Boy, I wanna tell you, that St. Eugene's is a hard school," I heard my father say rather nonchantantly while talking to a friend and swishing a drink. Hard school! Thanks, Pop! We all dreaded report card day. Who wanted to get chewed out in front of the entire class by the kindly Spencer Tracy/Father Brown turned grumpy Mr. Wilson/Father Brown? Teachers help, and so do subjects. With a crush on Sister Pauline, there wasn't any way I'd want to do poor schoolwork. Succeeding as a good student for my Irish nun was everything. I was determined to make at least okay marks. But Sister Pauline, as noted, was transferred. When I had a lay teacher in third grade, things didn't go as well. I was a cut-up, happy to make other students laugh at my nonsense. Then, Mrs. Butler put me in my place. "We have to listen to the class clown, again," she said firmly, finally noticing my childish behavior.

That got my attention. In fourth grade, a switch clicked on. This was the year we were introduced to American history. Innocent America still had legs to it. And I was hooked. This was Andrew Jackson history, Stonewall Jackson history. It was, also, February 12 and February 22 America, Abe Lincoln and the log cabin, George Washington and the cherry tree. Students furiously carved out those 19th century-style linotypes of each man. America was Pony Express history; The Gold Rush of '49 history, too. (That became my favorite. I'd stare at that color drawing of a 49er dipping his tray into a California creek, where gold particles, one assumed, would magically appear, making that long, hard trip from the cornfields all worthwhile.) And more. It was pre-Vietnam history, America winning all of its wars (seven for seven, I thought. Not bad). It was Paul Revere history, Nathan Hale and Patrick Henry history. Daniel Boone and Davy Crockett, Lee and Grant and the magnanimous surrender at Appomattox. Dolly Madison history (the War of 1812), Geronimo history and Amelia Earhart history too, as I sadly imagined her final flight across the Pacific.

Above all, it was, it seemed, Stonewall history. Andy Jackson. Stonewall Jackson. The world of 19th century America seemed like only yesterday. (A popular tune, "The Battle of New Orleans" by Johnny Horton on the radio and the great story of the young Hickory taking a lashing from a British officer rather than shining his shoes also had something to do with this.) Stonewall Jackson looked like Western North Carolina. Father Brown was the face of St. Eugene's. Stonewall was the face of Appalachia: long forehead, sad eyes, the long, full beard, the laconic, determined look: Mountain men, men of few words, determined to see it through. I was inspired by both Lincoln and Stonewall. Lincoln, too, had the sad eyes of mountain folk, as the war's enormous bloodletting had a profound effect on both Lincoln and Jeff Davis. Stonewall, too, was a winner. First Manassas, Cedar Mountain, Second Manassas, Fredericksburg. Winning! The South was going to win. Then, you turn the page— and there it was: Jackson being cut down by his own men in the wilds of Chancellorsville, Tar Heel men, no less. Jackson fell. He didn't survive. The South fought on. Gettysburg and Appomattox beckoned. Yes, it was possible to root for both sides. My family had its roots in the 1890s America. Stonewall and Lincoln. Grant and Lee (only I never bought that "war is hell" line from Sherman. I gotta believe he liked it and yes, folks were still sore about the March to the Sea). The novels to read here are *The Killer Angels* by Michael Sharra and *Shiloh* by Shelby Foote. Every Southern boy, in the course of their growing up years, goes through a Civil War phase. Why not? All of the major battles, save Gettysburg, were fought on Southern soil. The region, especially in Virginia and Tennessee, is dotted with battlefields, monuments, and cemeteries. Plus, the South was spared the Ellis Island immigration that took place before, during and after the war. As such, the percentage of Southerners who can trace their ancestry back to the war is far higher than in the Upper Sixteen. Then there are the casualties: Up North, one in eight white males of adult age perished; down South, it was one of four white males who died as a result of wounds or illness. (And to think that by my time, "white male" had become all-encompassing cuss words in American culture, a veritable name for evil.) Finally, the war itself was just too American for anyone to pass it up. The early Sixties represented the centennial of the war, an event that captured my imagination thoroughly. Plus, again, the battles were in the South, the place we now called home. The centennial celebrations, too, were entirely apolitical. America still had a sense of humor. Actors portraying Grant and Lee were "interviewed" by Walter Cronkite. The war was just American, American, American. Who is more American than Billy Yank and Johnny Reb? The early Sixties America that celebrated the war's centennial was a far more tolerant place. You could root for both. Billy was a brave and courageous soldier who fought for what he thought was right. Johnny, too, was brave and courageous, fighting for what he thought was correct. Southerners were taught to admire the tragic Lincoln. Northerners accepted Lee's loyalty to his home commonwealth of Virginia. Add in those gents, plus Grant, Sherman, Meade, Sheridan, and Chamberlain on one side: Davis, Jackson, Stuart, Forrest, and Johnston on the other. American, American, American. As Gertrude Stein correctly observed, nothing in American history will ever be as interesting as The Civil War.

So, the beginnings of a Lost Cause gene. Italians (my mother's side) have St. Anthony, patron saint of lost causes; Southerners had Robert E. Lee, dressed in full regalia, surrendering to the cigar-smoking Ulysses S. Grant at Appomattox. Why stop there? St. Eugene's represented a Catholic education. The Crusades, that bid to reclaim Christian lands in northern Africa, were next on board. I rooted my grade school heart out for those warriors the way I cheered on Stonewall or Mickey Mantle. First Crusades, fine; second Crusades, more good results; third Crusades, ugh, things got ugly, even though you had to root for those brave youngsters. Still, all of today's hand wringing over The Crusades never gets me down. The Rock will not break. Plus, The Rock, outside of the (mostly) non-believing West is doing just fine. As grade schoolers, our parents took us to mass each Sunday. My mother and I happily bellowed out, "Now Thank We All Our God," while my father, with seven dependencies, often knelt after communion with his head buried in prayer. A man of constant burdens. We had faith. Despite the Eighties-era sermons running down Ronald Reagan's Central American policies, I've kept it.

Alas, however, the story of the Church in the Sixties remains Vatican II. Where'd that come from? Who said the Church ever had to be relevant to the times? In his dramatic history, *Triumph*, Harry Crocker duly noted that such needless reforms were part of the heady optimism of the postwar era. The Forties were a war decade, the Fifties, a boom period. By 1960, abundance was in the air. So, too, was freedom, winds of change through decolonization, through liberation movements galore. The Church, incredibly enough, was also caught up in this optimism. In the early Sixties, nuns wore habits with big crosses around their necks. Priests said mass with their back to the flock (and towards Jesus on the cross). Every Sunday, the world's hundreds of millions of Catholics said the mass in the universal language, Latin, while sermons were delivered in native tongue. Women wore veils and once when they stopped, a new priest, Father Caldwell, gave a short, stern talk at the end of a mass, giving the ladies a good earful on the subject: Come back to church alright, but only with those veils back on. It's Church doctrine. Men wore suits and ties. Youngsters, too, imitated their parents' dress and habits. Again, we had to keep up with the Protestants: Wear your Sunday best.

At first, we thought the new dispensation was neat. The priest celebrating the mass while facing us, the liturgy in English. It took several years for the reality to sink in. The Church had now lost its mysticism, at least among prosperous Westerners. Vatican II was a disaster. It may be centuries until the Church fully recovers. I can remember the day when St. John Vianney Hall—home for young men seeking vocations—closed. The Catholic high school closed. The gym where we St. Eugene's Trojans took on other Catholic school teams before screaming crowds now belonged to Asheville-Buncombe Tech. Traditionalists such as William F. Buckley, Jr. and

Patrick J. Buchanan never stopped mourning the passing of the old Catholic Church, "militant and triumphant," as Buchanan recalled in his first masterpiece, *Right From The Beginning*.

By the Eighties, a new Catholic America was emerging. Nuns without habits took me a while to get used to (that lady just can't be one!). In the early Sixties, Catholics were considered cultural conservatives. Decades earlier, in the Forties, a great scare consumed East Coast Wasp-ish liberals. Such Protestants practiced birth control. Catholics—living in tight-knit, traditional and boisterous ethnic neighborhoods throughout the Northeast and Midwest— didn't. Catholics would out-breed Protestants and take over the country. But the Wasp still had power. Urban renewal, school busing, moving a sole minority family into white neighborhoods were all part of the plan to bring down conservative, Catholic America by pushing such folk from family-nurturing big city neighborhoods to sterile, television-watching suburbs (see E. Michael Jones's massive tome, *The Slaughter Of The Cities* for such planned disintegration). In 1961, no one knew where JFK stood on, say, abortion (it wasn't even an issue, the procedure was considered dirty, ugly, and immoral). By the Eighties, the face of American Catholic politics was now such men as Ted Kennedy, Tip O'Neill, and Mario Cuomo: Pro-choice, liberal Catholics all. Only a congressman from Chicago, Henry Hyde, seemed to stand for the old verities. Church attendance down, vocations down, school and hospital doors shuttered. The sad thing is that Vatican II began under the reign of Pope John XXIII, a much-beloved Italian-born pontiff, who as a boy, had slept in a stable among the animals. He, too, got caught up in the times. Still, the culture wars marched on. On battles such as abortion and school prayer, Southern Baptists were very willing to hoist a banner once manned heavily by Catholics. The Protestant South remained Christian, still. The South stood in opposition to modernity. It also leads the nation in charitable giving, with benighted Mississippi as the most charitable state in the Union. For decades, I've wondered if my fellow Southrons will ever know their place in the new America: A conservative, Christian people in a land more gnostic and progressive than ever.

IV

Patriotic Duties

"**H**ere. Take this. Read it." My mother tossed the sports page of *The Asheville Citizen* my way. My mother was pretty harried. Five young'uns running crazy around the house. Keep 'em busy. The headline was a jolt, "Braves Wallop Yankees, 8-3." Alright, it was only a 1963 spring training game, but it stung. I searched out the box scores. Couldn't read them. How am I going to keep up with Mickey and Roger? So, there's the incentive for reading. Box scores! Good enough. That led to other reading bouts in sports world: Tex Maule, Roy Jenkins, Curry Kirkpatrick and Mark Kram in *Sports Illustrated;* Dick Young, Leonard Koppett, Furman Bisher, Bob Broeg, Joe Falls, Jerome Holtzman, Jim Murray, and Art Spander in *The Sporting News.* Even *The Citizen* with Richard Morris and Larry Pope. My earlier reading habits, looking back, were mostly in journalism. Years later, I'd learn of the habits of the young T.S. Eliot, who plowed through the works of Shakespeare while his fellows were playing ball (Eliot claimed he'd rather be with his mates, but his protective mother kept him indoors).

Another young American who poured through The Bard as a teenager was Thomas Wolfe. Wolfe was Asheville's biggest star, bigger than Zeb Vance, whom Wolfe celebrated in *The Hills Beyond. Look Homeward, Angel* was Wolfe's first novel. Everyone in town knew about it. Even as a grade schooler, I liked the title. It was lyrical, melancholy, elegiac, the way a small town can be. Later, I'd learn it was lifted from a line from Milton's *Lycidas*. The town, more than ever, now claims Wolfe. In the Sixties, it did so, but gingerly, as many of the people Wolfe had satirized on the pages of the novel were either alive or had immediate kin still smarting from the young novelist's unintended wounds. Downtown, as it was in Wolfe's day, was the center of life, a place where business, politics, gossip, and nightlife came together. For the younger generation, the controversy was now the stuff of humor. A young man writes a novel and gets the entire town worked up in a lather. Whenever a teacher mentioned this in class, we'd break up laughing. Growing up, I didn't read it. Forbidden fruit. Intimidated, also, by its bulk. We had a neighbor, a Mrs. Hester whose lawn I mowed. Mrs. Hester, too, was an author. She was elderly and frail, but a portrait of her, young and wholesome, stood in her living room. She had a copy of *Look Homeward, Angel*. I opened it one day and fell upon the lines about Old Man Gant coming home from one of his drunken sprees.

O-ho—Godam

Goddam, Goddam,

O-ho—Goddam,

Goddam—-

I quickly slammed it shut. It did seem pretty funny and years later, when I read David Herbert Donald's biography of Wolfe, *Look Homeward*, he too mentioned those very same lines. "It was the first time I had seen a curse word in print," Donald recalled.

In the late Sixties, there was a television version of *Look Homeward, Angel* on one of the networks. My family gathered around in the den, sprawled out here and there, all watching religiously; one must; this, after all, was Asheville's famous son, books published in 31 languages. It was akin to a patriotic duty. (A London reviewer declared *Look Homeward, Angel* to be no less than the South's first contribution to world literature.) The 1957 stage version, written by Ketti Friggs, had won the Pulitzer Prize for drama. This show, however, was forgettable. All I remember was a scene where Eugene Gant (the adolescent hero based on the young Tom Wolfe) and his girlfriend, Laura James, both fibbed about their age: Eugene had said he was 18, Laura's given age was 21. Later, Eugene admitted he was only 16, while Laura sheepishly acknowledged she was 25 (not bad, Eugenics). In high school, Wolfe popped up again. He was part of an American literature reading list. I was an appallingly lazy student, reading only the latest issues of *Sports Illustrated, Sport* and *The Sporting News* and having no desire to plow through thick classics like *Look Homeward, Angel, Grapes of Wrath* or *Absalom, Absalom!* It wasn't a total waste. I lazily choose an "easy" novelist, Ernest Hemingway. *The Sun Also Rises* ended on a perfect note. *A Farewell To Arms* had many great love scenes, where Fredric, the wounded World War I ambulance driver, is being attended to by an Austrian nurse, Catherine. I buried myself in one of them while waiting for an early morning bus at Pritchard Park. "*I turned on her so I could see her face when I kissed her and I saw that her eyes were shut. I kissed both eyes shut. I thought she was probably a little crazy. It was all right if she was. I did not care what I was getting into. This was better than going every evening to the house for officers where the girls climbed all over you and put your cap on backward as a sign of affection between their trips upstairs with brother officers.*"

It represented a new way of doing things. (It worked for Frederic.) My friend Sandy Baker, to his credit, took on Faulkner, including that same *Absalom, Absalom!* We all had to do posters on our authors. Sandy's had a famous photo of a pensive Faulkner, pipe in hand, with Sandy's own question: Do you understand Faulkner? I don't. (Years later, my older sister claimed that she, too, had read Faulkner's tortured masterpiece in high school. That impressed me, made me wish I had the same wherewithal.)

The class included a film on Wolfe's life. It went by so quickly, just like the man's brief existence: Asheville, *Look Homeward, Angel*, Aliene Bernstein, death at a hospital in Baltimore. One novel, one girlfriend, a life in nowhere Baltimore. What a short, drab life, I thought. (Wrong. Wolfe only died in Baltimore at Johns Hopkins. I didn't know—or was too lazy to find out— that the stonecutter's boy wrote not one, but four thick novels, had more girls than Frank Sinatra and lived, not in dank Baltimore, but at several Manhattan addresses in swanky N-Y-C.) In time, 1975 rolled around. The year was Wolfe's 75th anniversary and Asheville was ready to take advantage of the big moment. The bookstores proudly displayed his novels. On a radio news report, Fred Wolfe, Tom's older brother, came up from Spartanburg for an emotional speech. "Tom," he said, speaking to a national audience. "Tom, can you hear me? You can come home again." It was all quite moving. (And that Fred was a helluva guy, defending his brother's legacy against all comers.) By then, my reading tastes were changing. From the papers and magazines to *Humboldt's Gift, Portrait Of An Artist As A Young Man, Notes From Underground*. Yes, Wolfe, like the poet Von Humboldt Fleischer in Bellow's Pulitzer Prize-winning novel had plenty o' girls. Fortunately (and happily) vocation time had arrived. Be a writer, try it. I was no jock, couldn't play guitar, wasn't a class officer. Yeah, try it.

So I did—and didn't—and did again. It took me some years to learn that reading and writing are joined at the hip. The process is never ending. It lasts through all those 50, 60 years or more of writing. That is, I had to give up my wonderful drop-out years and go back to college for an education in the humanities. But the reading days of the Sixties, leading into the Seventies, weren't a waste. *Sports Illustrated* was significantly more print-oriented. It contained plenty of color, but specialized also in long essays—-most prominently by the immortal Mark Kram writing on Jerry Quarry— that could produce many a memorable sentence. The Sixties, too, represented a heyday of the middle class. That meant not just the era of novelists, but also such middlebrow, high-circulation magazines as *Life, Look, Time,* and *Newsweek*. They, too, prided themselves on deep, learned and often entertaining prose. Yes, the world of *Sports Illustrated, The Sporting News, Life, Time,* or *Newsweek* did open up the world. Life wasn't so bleak and dreary after all. The world of almighty prose was the world of possibility. Who can forget the July

30, 1969 issue of *Life* on the Apollo 11 moon shot? Couldn't wait for it to arrive at our home address. (I already had been smitten. My teachers thought I had some expertise on the subject. They invited me to speak to upperclassmen on the entire Apollo project. I used miniature models to explain the docking and undocking, the touchdown and lift off process. I kept my eye on the plastic, not looking to see what my classmates thought.) There was the color cover shot of Neil Armstrong, Buzz Aldrin, and Michael Collins walking toward the giant capsule. Inside was Norman Mailer's narrative of the flight, excerpted from *Of A Fire On The Moon*. There also was James Dickey's always-energetic poetry; in this case, "Apollo," written in commemoration of the big flight. Poetry, for some reason, came hard for me. It took me years to digest it.

You look as though

You know me, though the world we came from is striking

You in the forehead like Apollo. Buddy,

We have brought the gods. We know what it is like to shine

Far off, with earth. We alone

Of all men, could take off

Our shoes and fly.

Mailer's muscular prose, on the other hand, grabbed my attention immediately. I admired the way he described the throngs at the lift off and the suburban sprawl surrounding Cape Canaveral, the venue for man's journey to the moon.

The radio was playing in the car. Fred Something-or-other from the Titusville Chamber of Commerce was talking fast. "And when the folks who were visiting this launch here go home, I want them to tell everybody how beautiful it was from Titusville."

"Folks," said the announcer, "get in on the Apollo 11 Blast-off Sale." The radio had lost no time.

America—-his country. An empty country filled with wonders.

Well, that was funny, too. The mass circulation slicks weren't always shallow. In a previous epoch, *Time* might feature William Faulkner (1938) or the great Virginian, Douglas Southall Freeman (1953) on its cover, introducing such giants to a large readership. I was introduced to Saul Bellow, John Updike, and John Cheever from cover stories in *Newsweek* and *Time*. There are worse fates. Should I have been reading Shakespeare and Dickens instead? Of course. Still, not a waste. In the future, a *Chronicles* here, a *Sewanee Review* there. Magazine reading turned into book reading, also book writing. Probably got it from my mother's side. My mother read magazines voraciously. My mother, also, had a great memory, punctuating long, informative monologues on child rearing with "I read somewhere" countless times, pausing and then going on to the next cachet of information, gliding effortlessly like a writer moving from paragraph to paragraph. Maybe the writing bug came from the Bruno side, also. My grandmother, like most women of her generation, did not attend college. Also like most folks of that generation, she grew up in the pre-television America when people wrote long, leisurely letters and journals. My grandmother loved to write those same long letters on loose leaf paper. My mother made sure all of us read those missives from Austintown. We lived a good 700 miles from our healthy grandparents. Reading letters was essential to keeping the family circle intact. Plus, this form of communication was far more fulfilling than long-distance phone calls where the talk centered around the weather and little else.

Our bookshelf, meanwhile, was typical for the times: Pearl Buck novels, JFK's *Profiles In Courage*, Albert Speer's *The Rise and Fall of the Third Reich*, Tolstoy's *War and Peace* (as Charles Murray wrote in *Human Achievement,* "Through the 1950s, an iconic list of the most important human accomplishments was part of American popular culture...It came to be widely accepted that the *Mona Lisa* was the greatest painting, *War and Peace* the greatest novel, *Venus de Mio* the greatest sculpture, *Hamlet* the greatest play, and Beethoven's *Fifth Symphony* the greatest musical work."), plus a neat stack of World Book Encyclopedia's, the 1966 edition. Most of all, to me, was the standard collection of Papa Hemingway: *The Old Man and The Sea* and *The Collected Stories*. Years later, my wife told me that her father, a humble man who worked his way into the middle-class, also had that same *Collected Stories* volume on the family bookshelf. Who didn't? That book defined the average American home. "I'd like to live long enough to write two more novels and one more collection of short stories. I know some pretty good ones." So wrote Papa in the introduction. Those lines were heartening to my impressionable young mind: You don't work at a job and retire; no, you write and write and write until, as Red Smith joked, you just keel over on that durn typewriter.

Hemingway was an exception. Again, the Sixties and Seventies reading wasn't literature, but journalism. Mailer was very good. So, too, were those sportswriters and not just in *The Sporting News*. In 1973, the Yankees celebrated their 50th anniversary of playing in Yankee Stadium, before a two-year renovation job took them to Shea Stadium in 1974 and '75. For the occasion, the Yankee management published a handsome commemorative issue inserted into their annual yearbook. Headlines throughout those decades proclaimed yet another title. (And naturally so. The aristocracy of American cities had the aristocracy of baseball teams.) Two stood out. In 1952, the Yanks overcame a three games to two deficit to defeat the Brooklyn Dodgers in the final two away games at Ebbets Field. The next year, they won their fifth straight World Series title: A record out of reach. In game seven of the '52 Series, the Bums, in the bottom of the seventh, had two on and one out. Casey Stengel, not playing the percentages, brought in a lefty, Bob Kuzava, to pitch to the lefty Duke Snider and the righty, Jackie Robinson. Kuzava had pitched well against Snider in the minors, hence the move. Snider flew out for out number two, but Robinson popped one up in the infield. With two outs and everyone running, the pitcher, the first baseman and even the Hall of Fame catcher, Yogi Berra, froze. Instead, Billy Martin came dashing in from second base to snag the ball and eventually win the game. The Bums had won two of three games at big, bad Yankee Stadium and *still* couldn't close the deal in the friendly confines of Ebbets Field. So, from the Oct. 8, 1952 *New York Daily News*, from the typewriter of the legendary Dick Young:

> They always said "it'll be a cold day in hell" before the Brooks win a World Series. It was cold enough yesterday, in the payoff scrap of the 1952 classic, but it must have been the wrong place because the Yankees—the indomitable, indestructible, insistent Yankees—won their 15th title and their fourth straight for Casey Stengel by copping the No. 7 scrap, 4-2, at the ulcer-factory known as Ebbets Field.

Well, I'd sing for my supper if I could write...Anyway, 1947 was when the Golden Age of Yankees-Brooklyn Dodgers-New York Giants dominated World Series games took off. That year, the Bums were beloved, but the aristocrats, again, prevailed. Or as Joe Trimble eulogized in the two-million-strong circulation *Daily News*:

> Brooklyn is a borough of three million pallbearers this morning. There, where the trees grow with equal vigor on the stately avenues of Flatbush and the sordid streets of Williamsburg, the citizens are deep in mourning. They've suffered their greatest loss—the world championship. With yesterday's 5-2 defeat in the seventh game of the Series, the dashing Dodgers died. They went down almost without a struggle under the crushing pitching of the Yankees' left-handed relief man, Joe Page, in the last of this mad set of games.

Sportswriting. Long may it live. I've spent the last 30 years trying to write leads like that.

Back to Wolfe. No, he wasn't the first, but Wolfe was vital, not the least his story of going from a paper boy on Valley Street to a world-famous author. Keep in mind that I punched out *Look Homeward, Angel* in two days and *You Can't Go Home Again* in one night, a long eight-hour reading bout in a room at the West 23rd St. YMCA. Wolfe's prose was the world of possibilities.

> They think I'm hell, thought Eugene, and they say I stink because I have not had a bath. Me! Me! Bruce-Eugene, the Scourge of the Greasers, and the greatest fullback Yale ever had! Marshal Gant, the savior of his country! Ace Gant, the hawk of the sky...Senator Gant, Governor Gant, President Gant, the restorer and uniter of a broken nation...George-Gordon-Noel-Bryon Gant, carrying the pageant of his bleeding heart through Europe, and Thomas-Chatterton Gant (that bright boy!), and Francois-Villon Gant...Edward-the-Black-Prince Gant...Czar-Ivan-the-Terrible Gant... Hercules Gant...Proteus Gant, Anubis and Osiris and Mumbo-Jumbo Gant.

His standing seemed secure. Into the Sixties, as the longtime and prolific Wolfe scholar John Idol has pointed out, up to 40,000 copies of *Look Homeward, Angel* were purchased each year. In the Seventies, you'd walk into any bookstore in America and under the "W" section in fiction, they'd be all lined up in a row: *Look Homeward, Angel, Of Time And The River, From Death To Morning, The Web And The Rock, You Can't Go Home Again* and *The Hills Beyond*. It seemed it would always be so. Decades later, *The Web And The Rock* went out of print. I felt the pit in the stomach. Can it be so? What happened? Was Wolfe too sentimental? Too romantic? Not politically correct enough? A victim of multiculturalism? Were his novels just too bulky for the television and now, digital crowd? Could he have been better served by expert editing? Was he too autobiographical? Yes, Wolfe had to get that Eugene Gant-George Webber saga out of his system. But he wrote many fine non-autobiographical pieces: The unfinished novella, *The Hills Beyond* about, as noted, the Vance clan; "Only The Dead Know Brooklyn," the immortal tale of man's time in this world as a permanent traveler, forever wandering the borough of parks and churches without ever knowing it "troo and troo" (as a 1947 edition declared: "It will live as long as the language"); "The Lost Boy," the grand tribute to the Wolfe's doomed older brother Grover; "The Web of Earth," the sustained comical and reflective monologue of Eliza Gant, a woman who brings children into the world, enduring the wonder and suffering such a life must entail.

Another Wolfe scholar, Hugh Holman, maintained that Maxwell Perkins, Wolfe's legendary editor at Scribner's, shares some blame. Perkins should have sliced up parts of *Of Time And The River* into shorter novels, *K-19* (about the rollicking train ride from Altamount to Boston) and *A Portrait of Bascombe Hawke* (a New England relative of Eugene Gant). Doing so would have revealed Wolfe as a master of short fiction. Doing so would also rank Wolfe as an equal of Hemingway, Faulkner, and Fitzgerald. Maybe young people would still read him. Maybe, too, the critics wouldn't be so harsh. Tempting (and Holman was a great scholar as I have long profited from his masterpiece, *Handbook To Literature*), but I must disagree. What? American letters without *Of Time And The River*? The world would be a lesser place. For years, I had pages 281-282 down pat.

> Immortal drunkenness! What tribute can we ever pay, what song can we ever sing, what swelling praise ever be sufficient to express the joy, the gratefulness, and the love which we, who have known and hunger in America, have owed to alcohol?
>
> We are so lost, so lonely, so forsaken in America: immense and savage skies bend over us and we have no door.

But you, immortal drunkenness, came to us in our youth when all our hearts were sick with hopelessness, our spirits maddened with unknown terrors, and our heads bowed down with nameless shame. You came to us victoriously, to possess us, and to fill our lives with your wild music, to make the goat-cry burst from exultant throats, to make us know that here upon the savage land, that here beneath immense, inhuman skies of time, in all the desolation of the cities...our youth would soar to fortune, fame, and love, our spirits quicken with the power of might poetry, our work to go on triumphantly to fulfilment until our lives prevailed. What does it matter then if since that time of your first coming, magic drunkenness, our head has grown bald, our young limbs heavy, and if our flesh has lain battered, bleeding in the stews? You came to us with music, poetry, and wild joy when we were twenty, when we reeled home at night through the old moon-whitened streets of Boston and heard our friend, our comrade, and our dead companion, shout throughout the silence of the moonwhite square: "You are a poet and the world is yours."

Don't drink and drive (Wolfe, as you might suspect, never had a license), but as Thomas Mann correctly observed, *Of Time And The River* is the great American prose work. Philip Roth once called Wolfe a half-genius, while Saul Bellow was a full genius. Yes, but Wolfe died at age 37. A longer life and he might have made it to full genius, even though I have no idea at how'd he react to the triumph of barbarism in postwar America. For decades, Wolfe's early death did not bother me. Look at what he left behind: four thick novels, three full-length plays, a bulky short story collection, two novellas, thousands of pages of published letters and two, giant-sized notebooks. But, yes, he died too young. For years, at least, it was a conversation-starter, especially with girls. All my pals, Gianelli in New York, Wazowski in Youngstown and Terry Harrell in Asheville would, at my hectoring, read that first novel and then give it back to me with the exact same solemn response: "You know, that's my life in there, Joey. That book is *me*." Dates didn't have the same reaction, even though they sighed over the Eugene Gant-Laura James love affair. Well, Wolfe, like Kerouac, is a guy's author, an introduction to a man's world of adventure and girls. Terry, like me, was full of hometown pride. He'd read from page one of *Look Homeward, Angel*—-"*Each of us is all the sums he has not counted: subtract us into nakedness and night again, and you shall see begin in Crete four thousand years ago the love that ended yesterday in Texas.*" Then he'd shut the book, gloating, "that is *so* much better than Hemingway! So much better!" What's the point of growing up in America without reading *Look Homeward, Angel* and *Of Time And The River*? Call it the sin of a wasted life. Yes, Wolfe has long been welcomed home in Asheville, but I had to move to the Seventies' New York to see how big he had once been. One Sunday evening, I was having dinner in an Italian restaurant. A middle-aged couple invited me over. We got to talking, the conversation going you-know-where. "After the war, *everyone* was reading Tom Wolfe," the husband announced. Yes, and consider the plaques at The Chelsea Hotel and on Columbia Street in Brooklyn Heights. I'd occasionally stand at the corner of West 42nd Street and Sixth Avenue, inside Grand Central Station or Penn Station, watching the manswarm pass by and think: Did any of these people grow up in the same town as the America's greatest prose poet? And if not, then what kind of life is that?

V.

EMPEROR OF LAWNS

The advantages of large families are many. One goes through life with an army of protection around them. You must be fast at the dinner table: So many hands, only so much food. Plus, at a certain age, you'd better go out and work. College? Well, pay for at least a part of it. My parents made a deal with us: We'll do the tuition, you have to pay for room and board. Sixteen did matter. Yes, you earned a driver's license, but as important, you could snag a real, taxpaying job. A W-2 form gig. That document was the passage to adulthood. It meant paychecks, legitimate bucks, something to stash away in a bank. Real money—-and the places that it might take you.

Most kids couldn't wait until 16. Little League was over, Babe Ruth League was winding down. It wasn't as much fun for the more slightly built boys, even though playing at McCormick Field, where Cobb, Ruth, Gehrig, Clemente and Stargell had all once dug in was a thrill. Thirteen was a good enough age to start earning dough. I wrote out around 20 letters, all indicating my desire to mow lawns and placed them in mailboxes all throughout the neighborhood. Sat back and waited for the flood of responses that, in fact, didn't come. Meanwhile, two of my older friends, Kevin Brennan and Mike Thompson, were ready to give up their two lawns, Mrs. Shipley's and Miss Miles's. They were glad to hand them over to this busher. One hot Indian summer Friday afternoon, all three of us met with Miss Miles. I was nervous. Kevin and Mike did the same two lawns together. Could I handle it? Miss Miles was a friendly woman who lived alone. She was a mountain woman with long hair in braids and a straw hat. She joked around with the two boys. (Mrs. Shipley turned out to be reserved, quiet and precise. She lived with her elderly husband. "Don't miss this spot near the patio," she'd instruct me. "Don't forget to rake under those bushes." Duties completed, Mrs. Shipley would allow for a thin smile.) The first day was a hot one. The grass was high, the motor would stall in the thick areas. Once Kevin and Mike left, I took over. And once the hill in the backyard was cut, the rest of Miss Miles's lawn came easy. I cut those two lawns into the fall, the best time of the year in Carolina. Pretty soon, I had the hang of it. It was like Kevin and Mike never existed. One Friday night, my friends rolled poor Mrs. Shipley's front lawn, toilet paper hanging from the trees, shaving cream smeared on the windows. Early the next morning, Mrs. Shipley called home and up I went, cleaning the front lawn. Yes, Mrs. Shipley could be precise, but she was such a nice quiet lady that I didn't mind the work at all. Plus, I felt grown up, dragging down the toilet paper with a rake, cleaning the windows with a sponge while my punk "friends" were snoozing, spoiled terribly by their easily intimidated parents.

In time, I had my own little empire. I'd trudge around the Grace and Beaver Lake neighborhoods with my lawnmower. Cars would stop and the driver would ask if I'd like to cut his lawn. I'd visit the house in question, take a long, authorative look over the yard and nod, yes. "How much?" the homeowner would eagerly ask. I'd give the lawn another going over. "Oh, I'd say ten dollars is okay." "Great!" Say what you will, some folks do *not* want to mow their own grass. This happened with several homeowners and right away, I'd see that it only took an hour to cut the grass. Ten bucks an hour. Much more, I reckoned, than the minimum wage in the United States. I had badly wanted a job with *The Asheville Citizen*. That—not lawn-mowing—was the ideal gig: A paycheck, an ID card, a position with the only daily in town. Plus, some friends had that job. I filled out an application to no avail. It didn't matter. I had a little empire up and down North Asheville, enough to keep me busy six days a week. Customers paid in cash, so I opened up an account at the Wachovia Bank on Merrimon. That, too, was a thrill. The balance in the little yellow passbook began to grow. My friends were impressed with the greenback collection. I wasn't looking for a car at 16, just a trip somewhere far away, namely the big city I had read about in the St. Eugene's library. Up the total went, hundreds to even thousands of dollars. Then one day—whoosh! —it was nearly all gone. I said nothing, knowing exactly what had happened.

It was my father's engineering job. Northrup, his employer, was feeling the pinch from a recent recession, plus cutbacks in military spending. The plant closed, my father was out of work. My mother remained a stay-at-home mom. Yeah, they had to rob my account. Ahead of us were long, anxious months. Seven dependencies and the man of the house out of work. I didn't know what to say or do. I was still a good three years away from a W-2 form job. I imagined my friends' parents, those in executive positions at banks and factories, offering my father a job. Like most sons, I was shy around my father. One evening, for some reason, I couldn't wait to see him. Maybe there was good news from school. I heard him drive up. I rushed to the door. But Pop just slipped by me without saying a word. I learned from my mother that he was on an interview for a big job. He learned that a competitor was Charlie, his best friend from Northrup, a fellow also out of work. We often visited the man's house out in Beaverdam. He didn't have a large family like us. Just the man and wife. My father and Charlie were genuine pals. Both liked fiddling around on their basement workbenches, hours on end. My father was unnerved by this competition between friends. On the way home, he had stopped off at St. Lawrence for silent prayer over the entire matter.

Meanwhile, my parents would stuff hundreds of envelopes with my father's resume inside. Every morning, there would be a stack of them on the cabinet by the front door. Hundreds of them! Couldn't just one of these fish bite? Indeed, they could. The job interview was in Buffalo. We all drove to the airport to see our father off. All I could think about was Buffalo and 12 inches of snow, months on end. The job didn't materialize. Instead, we did stay in Asheville. My father snagged a job as an engineer, first, for a condominium developer and later, at Walker, a manufacturer of automobile mufflers. It seemed a miracle to me. Buncombe County had 200,000 residents, "urban" for the South, but not so much anywhere else. How many engineering jobs could there be, especially now that the postwar boom was winding down?

My parents, I think, were glad. Yes, they were wary of the hillbilly folk, but who could give up on bucolic Western North Carolina? Plus, they had their circle of friends from the parish. On my mother's night to host bridge games, my father would hang out in the boys' room, while the ladies downstairs howled and howled away in laughter. "Listen to them laughing," my father said, amazed. He liked hanging out with his boys, but he was glad to see those ladies, all with 3,4,5,6 children or more, having some terrific—and I mean terrific—laughs.

My parents, too, were happy with my independent ways. I once cut a lawn for an old timer, a Mr. Wilson-type, up the block. He didn't like the job I did and told me so. I was fired, basically. Went home and told my folks. My father did not like that at all. Couldn't this old geezer see how industrious this chap was? I can still see my father storming out of the house, walking up the street to the old grump's place, his arms swinging John Wayne-style, full of purpose. He told that old man off, my mother told me. That I could guess. My friends remained impressed with my greenback growth. They wanted a piece of the pie, volunteering to help me if they got a cut of the pay. When I told my father, he was equally stern. "You're a professional," he said, wagging a finger. "Don't forget that." A professional. That might be correct. I had been mowing lawns for a good two years now and had the routine down: Mow half new grass, half grass already cut. Rake the loose grass, use clippers on the sidewalks and curbs. Sweep those sidewalks clean. A professional. Around this time, a lawn maintenance man named Jerry Baker was making the rounds, appearing in magazines and newspapers, at the bookstores and on television talk shows. I read Jerry's books, studied his gardening tips. Maybe I too needed a sharp white and green uniform just like him.

It didn't happen. I outgrew the lawn mowing jobs. The pay had its limits. Worse, my friend Mrs. Shipley passed away, dying suddenly of an aneurysm. I bravely attended my first wake, Mrs. Shipley sleeping quietly in a funeral home in West Asheville. For some reason, people murmured as I walked up the aisle on a school night. Miss Miles moved to Florida. Mrs. Shipley had been preceded by her husband and this, sadly, might have contributed. I often drove by the two houses, places of my first conquests, now populated by new inhabitants, melancholy that an era had ended. But not for long. I found another job. By ninth grade the disastrous effects of Vatican II were already in full force. The population at Catholic schools was shrinking. Plus, in a recessionary age, northern Catholic folk weren't moving down South in the same numbers. It was public schools from now on. Nineteen-seventy was the second year of full integration in the Asheville school system. Every ninth grader from North, South and West Asheville were bunched together at South French Broad, a formerly all-black high school near spacious Aston Park. I noticed how all the white kids from North Asheville and West Asheville hung out with their neighborhood crowd, while the brothers from all sides of town did the same. For now, only four or five of us from St. Eugene's made the jump to public school. We hung out as thick as thieves. All these strange faces, day in and day out. What to do? I tried out for sports, football and baseball. Did the drills, listened to the coaches, but all of a sudden, I was too small for this league. Cut! Just the word alone stings, like "fired." Sports was over—no glory, no cheerleaders—over!

It was back to work. I became pals with Dave Sutherland, another parochial school refugee. Dave had a job washing dishes at Grace Restaurant, a popular Greek eatery on Merrimon. Even in ninth grade, the teachers made a big deal about learning a skill, knowing that most of their working class charges, Afro and longhair alike, weren't going to college. Teach them a trade and when they dropped out (as hundreds of them did), they'd at least have a marketable skill as a mechanic or a hairdresser. Dave was like that. He wanted to be a restauranteur. The Greeks at Grace called him "the chef." I tagged along, taking on those big Greek pots every Sunday morning. After a few weeks, Dave palmed the job off on me. His mother had moved to Arden and he went to live with her. Dave, like Marky, was persistent. He'd eventually own his own restaurant at a mall in South Asheville. I visited him there once. It was hard work, running a restaurant.

Customers yakked away constantly. Dave was hassled endlessly over orders, checks, deliveries. Still, I was impressed. Dave had a dream—and he charged straight after it.

Sunday morning was the busiest day at Grace. The pots were full of mashed potatoes that stuck to the side. With dishes and silverware, you could count on the machine. With the pots, it was scrub, scrub, scrub. "I could get lost in one of those big Greek pots!" my pal Spiro Spironopolis joked one day at school. (Greeks in Asheville were tight, like, say, Albanians in The Bronx.) Either way, it was the three brothers and myself holding fort: Angelo, George, and Frank. Angelo was the oldest: quiet, bespectacled, he accepted his duties. George was the middle brother. Angelo and Frankie were stuck in the kitchen, but George was a maître'd of sorts. He was the face of Grace Restaurant, a caricature of his smiling plump face appeared in newspapers and flyers all around town. The backslapper, the glad-handler, George enjoyed his celebrity status. Frank was the unhappy brother. He was young and athletic but stuck every day in a hot kitchen. He wanted more out of life, namely his own restaurant in Myrtle Beach. I stayed clear of angry Frankie and only dealt with Big George. He paid in cash from the register. I was too shy to ask for what was mine by right: Namely, a free hot meal. When George saw me swipe a few mints from the counter, he got the message. In time, I closed the day with a hot feast of baked chicken, mash with gravy, hot rolls, a Coke, a salad, topped off by pe-cahn pie with whipped cream. This job ended with a bang, or more precisely, a splat—right in the eye. One day, I got dishwater soap in my eyes. I ran around the kitchen yelling like a banshee, "My eye! My eye!" as if I was blinded. A hot rag did the job. I ended up losing the job when George wanted to hire a vet down on his luck. He needed the job and I was odd man out. When I went back weeks later for a farewell meal with my folks and siblings, George was his usual gregarious self. He joked with my folks about the accident. "He ran around the kitchen," George laughed, holding an eye and mimicking his former dishwasher. "He thought he was blind." What's so damn funny? Christ, man, I put my eyeballs on the line for these boys.

More important, the magic age was approaching. Time for a real job with that W-2 form. Until then, the experiences at Grace held me in good stead. We lived next door to the Grove Park Inn, the before-mentioned world-famous resort hotel. In the Sixties and Seventies, Grove was only open part of the year, the summer and fall, but it was busy enough. On my first day, I was still shy. My boss was a temperamental German named Krauss. "Can I see Mr. Krauss?" I weakly asked a chef, a bearded young dude, mixing up a pot.

"Mister Krauss," he repeated, not looking up from the pot. "Heav-ey, heav-ey." Everyone called Krauss by his first name, Hans. The chef never gave me an answer. (We had a neighbor, Mr. Fillion, a Frenchman, who lived up the street. He taught the culinary arts at A-B Tech. Whenever I mentioned one of the chefs, including the bearded dude who snubbed me, Fillion would smile and grin, "I trained him, I trained him, too.")

The new job was fine. The crew at Grove was All-American: Summer workers bused down from D.C. and Philly, mixing in with mountain folk from Buncombe County. The city folk worked mostly as waiters. They rooted hard for such perennial losers as the Phillies and the Washington Senators. I was placed in the back with the dishwashing crew, mountain folk, people who dipped snuff the way the Southern Dems used to on the floor of the 1930s U.S. Senate. Having never seen such a sight before, I asked a kindly mountain woman, who like Miss Miles, kept her long hair in braids, what exactly she had in her purse. "Snuff," she replied. "I dip snuff. Want some?" Being a nice, middle-class boy, I shook my head no, didn't want my parents to smell such tobacco on my breath. The crew was supervised by an elderly German, who worked alongside his quiet wife and daughters. All this became the start of something weird, my attachment to the company of old folks, especially, later on, my maternal and paternal grandparents. The company of old folks fascinated me to no end. Why? I felt at ease with them, still too shy, I guess, around the co-eds. (All ya had to do was bring up music: The Stones, The Dead, The Doors, David Bowie, David Bowie, David Bowie, not this Mickey Mantle nonsense. Or as my uncle's girlfriend in Ohio once put me in my place when I brought up my hero, "Mickey Mantle is dead." Get the hint, boy. Get with the *Sgt. Pepper, Pet Sounds, Exile On Main Street* program.) The old German told stories about the Depression. Actually, I egged him on, now reading book after book about the New York Yankee era of Babe Ruth, Lou Gehrig and Joe DiMaggio, certain that this America in those books represented the final days of the real America, an age infinitely superior to these nihilistic times.

"What was it like, those days?" I'd ask the old man.

"Hard," he'd stared back at me intensely, hair slicked back, wire-rimmed glasses covering a now-pained face, but still pleased to be asked to reminisce. "Times was hard." He told a story that might have been common for those days, as I read a version of it years later in an Andrew Lytle essay. "You needed food for your young'uns," he continued. "The worst thing a Pa can hear is his children saying, 'Daddy, I'm hongry.' Folks would raid a corn field, a tomato patch. Farmers would look the other way. Them times was hard."

The dishwashing area was hot and bleak. I got the blues, wishing I was cruising Merrimon Avenue and Tunnel Road with my pals, chasing girls. So I finagled my way out of there to a janitorial gig with another old timer. He wore a white paper hat like a cook in a fast food joint. I wanted to be buddies and started donning the same cap myself. Occasionally, this old timer would allow a smile, but we never talked. He just wanted to be left alone to mop the floors in silence. It was fun, anyways. Once a week, the top brass took all of us, dishwashers and janitors alike, from our posts to the buffet line for a big deal they called "showtime." "Showtime!" some chef would yell and all the dishwashers got excited, repeating, "showtime, it's showtime!" They wanted to be out of that hot dishwashers area, too. What was showtime? We'd line up at the buffet station and assembly line-style, dress the plates with that evening's fare: Roasted beef, mashed potatoes, asparagus, hot rolls (for instance) all for a convention of The Georgia State Beer Association or The North Carolina Democratic Party. I couldn't stand showtime. What's the stupid deal? It's still a dumb ass dishwasher's job. Still, the old folks liked it. Showtime broke up the monotony of the long evening, pleasant Southern summer nights when everyone else was on the front porch swapping tales while us losers were stuck in a 100-plus degree kitchen. Plus, it was a matter of pride. Folks might be poor, they might not be going anywhere here at the end of their working lives, but at least they could put out a first-rate product of delicious food for the folks on the dining veranda.

Eventually, I started hanging out with fellows my age. There was Kenny Phillips, a 17-year-old from D.C. and Duane McDonald, a lanky kid from the outer counties. The three of us smoked, hosed down huge barrels of grub and in general, hung out while the clientele was still chowing down. Kenny was angry about having to stay in Asheville. He was from a broken home in D.C. and apparently too much for his mother. Duane was a country boy: Tall, pale, laconic. Ken couldn't stand the country boy company. He told D.C. stories: Parties, bands, women all that would put this hick town to shame. He looked down on us. Duane got the hint and began telling some stories, too. He came up with a tale about his pals and some girls in a mini-van (as Bill Clinton would describe it decades later, "a Southern deal" with astroturf in the back). One of the jerks came on to one of the girls. "I'm cool, baby,'" Duane repeated. "I was cool before you even thought about being cool," the brunette replied, wanting no part of the drunk punk. Duane's pal got nasty and made some smart aleck comment. Duane claimed that he stood up to the wise guy. "I told him to step outside," Duane recalled, now talking with a Clint Eastwood squint. "No man," he intoned, "cusses at a woman in front of me." It was dead silent in the trash can area. Kenny got the hint. Be tough, too, around this cat. It worked. From then on, Phillips treated Duane as an equal. He'd even blush once or twice while in his company. The two became pals, back-slapping, soul shakes, wrestling around, smoking and joking. I was the odd man out. What tale could I come up with? I was no fighter, just a few slapdash brawls on the playground and in the Y locker room. Summer came and went. In the fall, Duane went to one of the county high schools. I was back at Vance High. One day, I ran into Phillips in the packed hallways. I didn't have many friends in high school, so I was glad to see a mate from the dishwashing crew. "Kenny! How ya doin'?" I grinned and gave him a big slap on the back. He didn't like that at all. He got flustered. "I knew you'd do that," he fumed. "You seen me, you got to say it in front of everybody?" He made a move but backed off. Was glad he did. Phillips was older and bigger than me. To lose a fight would mean total humiliation. I'd have to drop out. Instead, he spun around and disappeared into the crowd.

Who was Phillips, anyway? Just one of the 1,001 nobodies at VHS. He hated being there. He missed D.C., all his street buddies. He was stuck in this hillbilly town, this strange mix of longhairs and Afros. Worst of all, he was forced to fit in by having to wear a jean jacket instead of the brown or black leather folks dealt in up North. Hell, even the brothers wore jean jackets, like a bunch of damn rednecks. That was the last time I saw Phillips. Either he moved back to D.C. or just dropped out, a day or two of VHS being all he could take. No one knew him when he was there, no one would know he was gone. Plus, Phillips was 17, a good year past the legal drop out age. I never saw Duane again, either. And I don't think any punk cussed at a girl in front of him.

Grove Park Inn was my first full-time summer job. We worked late hours, 4 p.m. to midnight, six nights a week. It led to the start of bad habits. My feet were too sore at night for me to get any sleep, so I developed a lifelong nocturnal habit of watching late night TV, which in the Sixties and Seventies was all Johnny Carson and later, The Tom Snyder Show. Grove Park, as noted, was closed in the fall, so I had to find something else when school started. Sixteen at last! The Grace and Grove jobs were off the books, but the gig at Burger Heaven was legit, the W-2 form job I had long desired. It was an easier gig and not unwelcome either, especially after all the yelling and cussing and clanging going on in the hot kitchen. There were no angry teenagers, no melancholy old timers, either. Burger Heaven! A burger joint. Great choice! Grease and french fries too. After a while, your face looks like a.... But all the fellows got along. These jobs, blue collar or pink collar, represented the corporate bond individualism that my later mentors, such as Richard Weaver and M.E. Bradford would hail as the Southland's great bulwark against an atomistic world. It was a place where everyone looked out for each other; almost like an extended family. I was stuck up and haughty (a bit like Phillips myself) with all this matter-of-fact, know-it-all talk about the big city. My co-workers put up with it. (They may have been amused, but not jealous as NYC's reputation in the Seventies was in the pits.) Curtis, a twenty-ish fellow, was the supervisor. He was more than just a nightshift manager. He had a young bride at home that we never saw. Curtis also saw himself as a pillar in North Asheville, a businessman dedicated to the community's well-being. As rush hour approached, he'd stand alone, hands in pocket, in front of the joint, watching the commuters buzz by on Merrimon. I never knew what he was thinking but assumed that he saw himself as a protector of sorts, giving hot food to the community, serving as a mentor to these would-be Richard Petty's, an older brother/father type to the young ladies, themselves several years ahead in maturity over the crew of boys they would, someday, have to tame into being men. Once, my folks and siblings came in for a weeknight meal. "Why don't you go out there and say hello to them?" Curtis asked. "Ah, I don' wanna. I see 'em every day," I sulked back, teenage-style. "Son," he rebuked, "don't talk that way. They are the only parents you are ever going to have." And that's how he was. He wanted to relate to each of his charges on a personal level. Curtis knew folks were moving down South. He had solidarity with working people everywhere. When I told him my maternal grandparents were from Youngstown, he just looked at me and said, "steel mills." When I said my paternal grandfolks were from West Virginia, he stopped again: "Coal mines." I nodded both times.

Above all, Curtis was an Asheville patriot. He was friendly to the cops, giving them the standard freebies: Burgers, fries, soda. The cops had their squad radios on and huge heaters packed onto their belts as they shot the breeze with their pal. For police, they were laid back, at ease. Asheville, as compared now to America's condition, was a fairly low-crime town.

Curtis stayed on in the business. A good decade later, he had moved to another burger joint, one closer to the edge of town. He looked the same and seemed, as always, in control. He put his hands in his pockets, bounced back on his feet and asked what I was doing.

"Teaching," I said (at nearby A-B Tech). "Teaching," he repeated back, hands still in pockets. I think he was glad that his boys were moving on in the world. At least I hoped he was.

The job, at the same time, was like the others. My mates were fellows I had played ball with in Little League or the Y League. There was the same pattern: Fellows got promotions, raises. They married their high school sweethearts. They soon had enough of school. Those that stayed went to A-B Tech or UNC-A or to a better-paying job at a mill. The proprietor was Mr. Dandy, a precise, reserved man, a northern transplant also, someone who warily regarded these uncouth country boys charged with the upkeep of his burger franchise. Often, Dandy worked alongside us. "Always repeat the orders, boys," he'd insist. So when a cashier announced, "three cheeseburgers, two french fries, one chocolate milk shake, one coke," he'd pronounce the order back, word for word, like a diligent schoolboy. Dandy had a congenial streak. He'd always pick me up whenever I hitchhiked my way around town. He drove a sleek, little gray Mercedes, one so cool that I'd always slam the door shut after the ride. "I told you, don't slam the door." Eventually, the eff word made it in between the "the" and the "door." My coworkers claimed that he'd spy on us from a parking lot across the street. He'd sit in the parked car, lights off, as we teenagers frittered away the closing hours. That bad? Duffy's wife, on the other hand, was a nice lady, a peppy little New Yorker who knew her husband was a grouch. She loved Curtis, always giving him a hug and a kiss and in general, keeping spirits up. With the exception of fancy Atlanta, big league sports hadn't arrived yet in the southeast, so all the fellows were huge college sports fans: Bama in football, UNC in hoops. I was a Tar Heel fan, too, but football was different. For the first time, I began to feel like an outsider. I was a teenager now, of legal age and there was a slight identity crisis involved. Who was I? A Tar Heel? Or maybe an "Italian-American?" The latter was "in" now, what with *The Godfather* movies, *Serpico*, plus television cop shows like *Columbo*, *Barretta* and *Toma*. I read all the paperbacks. The saga of the Corleone's, with the family hierarchy, was so moving you'd forget that they were criminals. Plus,

I was already mourning the passing of the New York of Joe DiMaggio and Yogi Berra. My maternal grandparents with their accents and fluency in the language of Dante and Petrarch moved me, also.

Things came to a head when Notre Dame played Bama in two big Sugar Bowl games. There was the Crimson Tide with the great Paul "Bear" Bryant, the most beloved Southerner since Robert E. Lee. Then, there was my father's favorite team, the Notre Dame of Johnny Lujack, The Four Horsemen, Knute Rockne, Frank Leahy, Paul Hourning and the "Touchdown Jesus" mural on the library, facing Notre Dame Stadium. On this subject, reader, I was my father's son. Me and big mouth, I bet with Curtis and the other fellows on the '74 and '75 Sugar Bowl games, which the Irish both won by close scores. Curtis would hand over the bucks and write in large letters, "ALABAMA IS #1" on the greenbacks. The chiefs got their revenge, making "Scotchie" work the 12 noon to 8 p.m. shift on summer weekdays, while Mickey and Spike and the other fellows were out on the town with their 395 SS Chevies and their little brunette girlfriends. It wasn't that bad. Mrs. Dandy said I made "the best french fries in town," which gave me a swell head, since when I started, I got bored with dressing cheeseburgers and wanted to do something different. And who cares about long hours? Mickey, with a blonde on the side (his promotion—not to mention, the green hog—impressed the ladies), often let me go home early. Again, I was a UNC fan in basketball; the Notre Dame stuff was forgotten offseason. Mickey and Spike and Curtis seemed genuinely glad when I got over my self-centered shyness and had a few dates of my own. Either way, the longer hours meant bigger paychecks, more dough for the yellow bank book, more money, in all, for that summer big trip to bucolic 1973 NYC.

Mowing lawns, washing dishes, slinging fries. What did it all mean? First, there is no such thing as a bad job. Any job is a good one (The boss may be an s.o.b. If so, outwork the bastard.) In time, I'd read Saul Bellow's best short story, "Looking For Mr. Green" about a Depression-era classicist who can only find work as a welfare check deliverer for the city of Chicago. Mr. Grebs performs his duties diligently, if not successfully; the story's epigram was culled from the Old Testament: "Whatsover thy hand findeth to do, do it with thy might..." Yes, the little yellow bank book was the ticket. Next thing you know, I'm trading in bucks for traveler's checks, for an airline ride to the big city (if some punk tried to roll me, the traveler's checks were still in my name.) After that, the Keane's home in Forest Hills, the D train to my dream borough, The Bronx, for a few games in the final year of the real Yankee Stadium (1923-1973).

All of this had a practical side. Working and saving money was a decent habit. You learned to get to a job on time, to take orders, perform duties, earn a paycheck and save money for tuition. It led to middle-class habits and middle-class prudence. I was well aware of my father's graduation from the family business to the big, vast American middle class. My generation would, at the least, have to do the same—-and after the recessionary Seventies, the middle class would never be so easy to attain as it was in the 1945-1972 Baby Boom era. Still, whatever happened to youth and glory? Had to waste my twenties on something. The savings book was still king. Now it was money not for a vacation in the big city, but for other pressing matters: Tuition, down payment on that first home, a monthly allowance if needed, an inheritance fund and—-hold on, not finished! A property tax fund (thanks Noo Yawk!). You want your children to remember you fondly, don't you? If they don't, who will? Love yes; but better, money. Not for luxury, just for middle-class survival. So save, save, save, right to the end. It becomes a lifelong credo: No HBO on the idiot box, drive slowly in the right lane, let the morons pass, ration food and gas, live at home during those college years, stay at a Y in your NYC years, instead of a one room flophouse. It all went back to those exuberant days in the late Sixties and early Seventies, getting out of the house and into the working world, all for the benefit of the little yellow bank book for deposit at that handsome brick building on Merrimon, the ticket to the wide world beyond the mountains.

VI.

A Place On Earth

One paycheck America, too, had its charms. With dad as the sole breadwinner, mom could stay at home and hopefully, raise normal children. In the summer, that meant no stowaway camps, either. For us, summers meant a month in bucolic-turned-suburban Austintown, hometown to my folks. My mother was homesick for family. My father liked the arrangement too, because he could have the house to himself, doing chores while booming his favorite music on the Hi-Fi. Our roots were in Ohio. Austintown, outside of industrial Youngstown, remained home to both my maternal and paternal grandparents, plus aunts, uncles, and cousins galore. So off we went in late June, a two-day drive from the hardscrabble two-lane road Southland to the sleek, four-lane interstate highways of efficient Yankeedom. We drove past Cherokee country, full of tents with smoke rising from them, through more mountains and into Kentucky, where I eagerly stuck my head out of the window, believing that once we crossed the state line, the grass would indeed be dark, Duke Blue Devil *blue*. I was disappointed when it was as green as Tennessee or Carolina turf. On through London, Kentucky and Paris, Kentucky, hours of two-lane driving now past the one-story shacks in Covington, Kentucky to——magic! —-efficient Yankeedom and mighty Cincinnati, Ohio, where little Crosley Field was lit up for night games. These two-day journeys represented trials of great endurance. Seven and later, eight of us in one Carolina blue Ford station wagon (my father dropped us off and picked us up weeks later). We struggled to find space to snooze in Cincinnati and to deal with a bloody nose in Columbus, before driving through Sherwood Anderson country to Youngstown itself.

Ohio! Sherwood Anderson country was green and hilly, like Western North Carolina, but much of the state was flat and hot, redeemed by acres of cornfields. At the same time, it was now a violent zone, entering North from South. In the late Sixties, Northern cities were burning, dozens at a time. In 1967, we made the trip the same time that Detroit went up in flames. It was an eerie feeling, knowing that several hundred miles west of little Austintown, a once-mighty American city ("the arsenal of democracy") was being burnt. President Johnson was on the radio. "We have just gone through a week that no nation can endure for long," he intoned solemnly (as I best recall). My father just reached over and flicked it off. Was glad he did. A far cry from JFK and all of those joke-filled afternoon press conferences! Every time I heard the words, "President Johnson today said..." on the radio, I felt the pit in the gut. Not him again. Bad news was in the offing. More clicks off. The next year, 1968, saw more rioting. After the King assassination and into the summer, it was expected. The U.S. Capitol Building, as the media breathlessly reported, was being protected by federal troops for the first time since the Civil War. Sheer anarchy was in the air, staying that way until the early Seventies, when the Vietnam War ended. I remember an incident outside the Seven Mile Inn. One hot afternoon, two cars smashed into each other. Out of one car came a middle-aged white male, sunglasses on and fuming. Out of the other came a black woman, shades on too. "You were flyin'!" the man said. "I wasn't 'flyin'," the lady responded. All around was twisted steel, broken glass, steam rising from the radiators. It is good, I thought, that this is happening way out in the middle of nowhere. Just think if it had taken place on a street corner in Youngstown, Cleveland, Toledo, or Dayton. The whole damn city might have gone up in flames by nightfall. That, too, was the Sixties.

Family was the reason we traveled. My maternal grandfather emigrated from Italy to the U.S., via Canada. Why? Well, his older brothers had done the same. He decided to join them. No talk of freedom. Grandpa Bruno missed Italy (Foggia, on the eastern seaboard, was the family stump) terribly. He spent years wondering if The Big Move had all just been a mistake. A second niece, Lisa Iagulli, once wrote a poem about him.

Great Uncle Julius,

Always plowing

His acreage; pepper

Tomatoes

For sauce

He greets us with open arms

Ah, *paisano*!

Vino? You must drink!

Red wine, rose, all homemade

At dinner, he and Grandpa

Rattle on in Italian gibberish

I watch their hands, faces,

Smile; I don't know what

They're saying, but

I understand

Too much food

Pasta, fried peppers, more vino

Mangia! *Mangia*!

He talks about the homeland

Stories

His brother once had to put a turtle

In his mouth to hide it from Mama,

And swallowed it!

I've heard the story before

The same cackling laughter and

Italian curse that follows

Great Uncle Julius

He lives in Youngstown

Somewhere in Italy

In 1958, he visited his homeland. There were black and white photographs of brothers, cousins, and town folk. But that was the only visit. Life was in Austintown, with his wife, daughters and brothers, especially Tony, who always arrived at the five-acre homestead in a shiny, black roadster, dressed to the nines in a pinstriped suit and tie, like Joe DiMaggio entering Yankee Stadium. Only one brother, Romeo, stayed behind. He visited Austintown one summer. This patch of northeastern Ohio was turned into a backyard in Foggia: Picnic tables, pasta, salad, wine, and bocce ball. "Come on, Julie, c'mon. We need this score," relatives would encourage my grandfather as I tried to make sense of this alien sport.

My Grandfather Bruno was older than my grandmother and the dominant personality of the two. Again, no favorites. My maternal grandmother was a quiet, little woman who dutifully manned the counter at the grocery store. My grandmother indulged in my great interest for baseball cards. In time, Grandma B, too, got excited when a new shipment came in. "Here they are," she'd tell me smilingly, as I looked in vain for another Mantle or Maris card. Even when I was young, I knew my grandmother had a hard life. We kept a photo of Grandma Bruno's family on our living room bookcase mantle. She was the youngest of a large clan with four older brothers of which only one, Uncle Mark, was known to us. My grandmother looked exactly like my younger sister, Marybeth, a young lady highly popular among all my pals. (That's why they became friends with me. Wanted to meet my sis.) In the picture, my grandmother held her mother's hand, a sure point of compass in a hostile world. Sadly, it didn't last. At a young age, only 11, my grandmother suffered the loss of her mother to an illness we were never told about. Never asked, but I don't think Grandma B ever recovered. My grandmother grew up in Youngstown and graduated from Rayan High School during the city's Ellis Island days. In time, Grandma B married and bore three children. There were the usual behind closed doors scenes. Once, my mother and her sisters got all upset over a pair of gloves and who they belonged to. My grandmother, according to family legend, just took those gloves and tossed them into the oven, settling the issue once and for all. It was a happy family, as the neatly laid-out photo albums illustrated.

My Aunt Diane showed an inclination for learning, hoping eventually to attend college, something still unusual for a young woman in the Fifties. My grandparents, like most Americans, never attended college, but they saved money to send their second daughter there, after which she enjoyed a long teaching career. We even managed to have some fun. One New Year's Eve, 1966, the adults went out on the town. My siblings turned in early, while I stayed up with a James Cagney flick on prohibition. It scared me good. Moonshine was everywhere: In the wooden barrels, stashed in the back of trucks, even being poured in the bathtub: Wise guys with machine guns rubbing each other out left and right. It went on past midnight. I got plenty drowsy and a little paranoid, too. My grandmother walked into the living room to see how I was doing. Grandma B's appearance startled me. Didn't know what to think. Finally, I blurted it out. "Grandma," I asked. "Are you drunk?" Yes, my little grandmother, a devout Catholic who never missed Mass—

drunk! Well, everyone else was—at least on the idiot box. Plus, it *was* New Year's Eve. That gave my grandmother a good smile. Later on, it was an occasion for some belly-aching laughs. "And little Joey asked me—he was so serious—grandma, are you drunk?'" My mother, my father, my aunts and uncles, my siblings, and Grandpa Bruno, too, all howled on. I felt like a moron for even asking.

My grandmother's life was hard. She was orphaned by her mother's death. Grandma B persevered like any good Christian: Living for others, for my grandfather, her daughters and those nine grandchildren. Grandma B put together some great photo albums. One was of immediate family life. My grandparents, my mother and my aunts making their way to what seemed like a normal life: Holidays, birthdays, snow ball fights, first communions, confirmations, classmates and boyfriends. Youth and frolic in the incredulously happy America of the late Forties and early Fifties. Turn to the final page and there was my older sister and myself posing for a baby photo. An era had ended, a new one had begun. Later, I stumbled across a smaller photo book, "Grandma's Brag Book." There, Grandma B's grandchildren romped through their own childhood. That made me feel better. Plenty of fulfillment in this life, after all. Years later, when I introduced my future bride to the Ohio folks, a great aunt whispered, "your grandmother would like her." I knew this would be the case, but hearing it was reassuring nevertheless.

Both of my grandfathers' ran their own businesses, another fact that impressed me greatly. The paternal side was West Virginia and coal mines; maternal side, Youngstown and steel mills. Grandfather Bruno had health problems. There was asthma, a combination of steel mill life and effects of fighting in the trenches for the Italian Army in World War I. So he left Oakland Heights (the "dago hill" of Youngstown) for Austintown, where, as noted, the family operated a grocery store and where my grandfather moonlighted as a bouncer in a local Italian restaurant. I didn't like the grocery store as much as the Seven Mile Inn, the saloon my paternal grandparents ran. During dinner hours, my grandparents and their three daughters would take turns to man the counter when a customer interrupted the meal. It could be tiresome. Still, it was home. In fact, the backyard, many acres itself, was a Little Eden with woods, creeks, and meadows. Inside, the trucks rushed past at night as I tried to sleep. My grandmother saved a pack of baseball cards for me. She also left me alone when I watched the Bombers win an easy, late 1963 blowout over the Detroit Tigers on the Game of the Week on the little black and white television set. (How easy this looked! Yankee Stadium in its splendor, a Yankee win, a Yankee pennant. The world spun perfectly on its axis.) But as my grandfather reached his mid-60s, the job became too onerous. So they sold the store to Zinck's Aluminum Siding and moved up Mahoning to five acres on Canfield-Niles Road. They didn't retire. My grandfather set up a nice bed of produce, selling a brisk business of peas, corn, radishes, and strawberries in the summer, while spreading manure on the lot during Ohio's long winters. During my own aimless, drop-out youth, I spent a good seven months from winter to fall of 1977 in Austintown. I'd help spread manure. "Put your heart into it," my grandfather would urgently appeal, holding his chest. "You *must* put your heart into it."

My grandparents did this for a good 25-plus years. At age 90, my grandfather, now a widower, could sit on the back porch and gaze out proudly on another planted bed of corn. It was an amazing achievement, akin to being a character in a Wendell Berry novel. My grandfather was still in Italy, but he lived the old Jeffersonian ideal, the life of free landowners in a free republic, too.

My maternal grandparents spoke Italian around the house. However, they forbade even the teaching of it to their daughters, reasoning that if this was America then English, even in the privacy of one's home was in, while Italian out. That was a little harsh. Italian, after all, is the language of Dante and Petrarch, the most lyrical of the Romance languages. Speaking it at home was no threat to the American Way (which Italian immigrants happily assimilated, wanting no part of affirmative action or bilingual education.) My paternal grandparents were different to me, they seemed more American. My grandfather there traced his ancestry to the late 19th century, making me feel that I, too, was part of the old America.

His father came from Slovakia before it was part of Bohemia. Why? Who the hell knows. Freedom? It wasn't being denied over there. Edward Luttack once wrote that Eastern Europeans only flooded into America once they learned how easy it was for the workingman to buy a Model T. That made sense. The Scotchie men loved cars. My grandfather used to trade in his new Caddy every year for the latest brand. My father loved autos, too, even just tinkering under the hood in the garage, hours on end. My great grandfather died when I was 13. I never knew him; just remembered the home movies of a gray-haired man with a huge mustache, someone attractive to my mother. My paternal grandfather was like me—or more to the point, I was like him. In the Twenties, he read the novels of Zane Grey and decided to make a new life out West. He left Clarksburg, West Virginia as a teenager and made it as far "west" as Warren, Ohio. There were stories of him sitting in a hotel room, lonely and melancholy, like the young Vito Corleone in the opening scenes of *The Godfather, Part II*. Other stories, this one from Uncle Bob, had him going back home, telling his father that he had had enough of the open road, now he was willing to go to college. "No, you cannot do that!" my uncle related, regaling a small crowd, imitating his grandfather's stern voice. "You must go to work in the coal mines!" Was it true? My great grandpop, to me, was a mellow old man. I just listened, thinking: *This is the blood that runs through your veins. If you ever have children, try to suppress it.*

And so, it was back to Warren, steel mills, marriage and six sons, all tumbling out in the Depression Thirties and the wartime Forties. In the latter decade, the Warren mill went on strike and all the workers got canned. My grandfather had saved some money: He and a partner opened a hotel and restaurant in Lake Milton. But my grandfather, I think, was too independent to work with any man. He sold his share of the hotel and bought the Seven Mile Inn in Austintown. Why the name? It was located seven miles, exactly, from the Youngstown city line. The history? In the Twenties, it was a speakeasy, busted and re-opened several times over. There was no place on earth I loved more. (This was true for my brother and my Florida cousins.) Like the grocery store, it was rural. Every morning, you could hear the birds singing, while smelling the sweet creek water. The woods were positively picturesque in snow. In fact, it was another Eden. The Inn lasted much longer than the hotel. My family owned it from 1948 to 1999. They had broiled hot dogs and Seven Up. No place, indeed. Since my grandparents purchased it in the late Forties, just entering the house attached to the bar area was like walking back in time, to a better place, to the happy nation of Steve Van Buren, Johnny Lujack and the 1948 World Champion Cleveland Indians. There were books: A history of the baseball New York Giants by the immortal Frank Graham, an engrossing picture history of the The Tribe. Giants! Indians! When the Tribe made it to the 1997 World Series and lost in the damn extra innings of the seventh game, I wrote Uncle Bob a letter of condolences. When, in the late Nineties, we entered The Inn for my grandmother's funeral, The Tribe were playing the Red Sox in the American League playoffs. Uncle Bob and I wanted to get away from it all. He was alone in the small television room, rooting hard for the Indians. I joined him, just like old times. The score was 2-0, Sox. Later, with two men on, Dave Justice nailed a three-run homer. My uncle cheered. I cheered. We exchanged high-fives. For years, a photo of Joe Gordon hung on the barroom wall. How I wanted those damn Injuns to win a World Series! Just once. For my uncle. For my late grand dad, too.

The Seven Mile Inn was a second home. I liked the manly smell, the world of jockery. My grandfather would sit in his bedroom, counting the checks and greenbacks, pile upon pile, impressing us greatly. "My God," my father would blurt out admiringly. (He was still a salaried worker.) I liked to brag that my grandfather sent six boys to college on The Inn's dough. His old man wouldn't let him go to college. No way would he make that mistake with his boys.

So Ohio, like the Grove Park Inn, was the world of older folks: Specifically, the world of grandparents. I considered myself lucky just to have known them for so long. It was a blessing, especially growing up in a mobile nation, where young people, if they know their grandparents at all, only know that they live hundreds of miles away, visiting at holiday time only every now and then. Plus, I was looking for wisdom, for an easy relationship. The Robert Penn Warren poem got it right. "I like talking to you, grandpa. You tell me things." I was close to both of my grandfathers. Grandpa Bruno thought that my father was too hard on me (I didn't). He even wanted me to come live with Grandma B and him. "Come live with us," he'd say, excitedly. "We'll buy you shoes. Treat you right." He was damn serious, but I wanted to be home. Plus, my father had a license over his offspring. (I didn't want to live with my grandfolks and be spoiled.) My mother was homesick. Working on the five acres was good for my mother's conscience for living so far from home. The Inn had hot dogs and soda. I could sit with Grandpa Scotchie, eat and drink by the huge fan, the two of us watching The Tribe struggle through another mediocre year. I wanted grandparent wisdom. But he was quiet. He'd tell his friends that I looked like my Uncle John, which made me feel good. Maybe someday I could be a real Scotchie male.

A decade later, in my wasted youth, I spent the summer of 1977 with them. We'd mow grass in the backyard. My grandfather badly wanted to do yardwork, but the years were piling up on him. "Don't grow old," he'd growl at me. "Shoot yourself first!" So, I gladly mowed the lawn (my specialty, anyway). Grandpa S played cards with the fellows, kicked out any pool hustlers from the big Saturday night tournament. He helped from behind the bar when necessary, but he, too, had a license over me. During a grade school visit, he once scolded me for not eating well. I sat by his left side at the table, scarfing down the meat and potatoes, but not the tomatoes or cucumbers. Didn't like them, so why eat the vegetables? Big mistake. One night, my grandfather had enough. "Eat them," he ordered. I was petrified. Surely, he was joking. I looked around the table at Grandma S, aunts and uncles. They all stayed silent. Who's the man of the house? "Eat them," he repeated, pointing to the greens. "Eat them, now." By now, tears were flowing. Again, no help from the rest. A spoiled boy who doesn't eat his greens. In my wasted, drop-out years, I had it coming some more. My parents were anguished at me for seemingly throwing my life away. There must have been some communications between Asheville and Youngstown. "I just don't know what's wrong with that boy," I could now imagine my father telling Grandpa S. If so, I was in for it. A boy upsetting a man's oldest son.

After my seven-month stay in 1977 Youngstown, I headed back to Asheville. My pals had a farewell bash at The Inn. After the backslapping and palm slaps ("See you in New York, Joey!"), my grandfather took me aside. A limp handshake. "You're a man," he said up close. "Start acting like one." What? A man? No lectures here, grandpop. I lived those years on my own in the big city, right there in the middle of Manhattan, manual labor job after job, rent on time, food in the belly. That's N-Y-C pal, not little Warren. A "man" my eye. Of course, I didn't say such things, just took what was coming my way. The old man was correct. After flittering away the Seventies, it was back to college: Degree, teaching, journalism, marriage: Back to the middle class that I came from and to where I belonged. Who knows? Maybe my father had a conversation with Grandpa S about my wake-up call (well, I did plenty of reading during my bohunk years). Don't know. Either way, Grandpa Scotchie came to my wedding in the now-late Eighties New York. Near the end of his days, my grandfather had wanted to see his oldest son, maybe he wanted to see the big city 'fore it was all over; maybe, I hoped, he was glad a grandson had quit causing his parents years of anxiety. Don't know that, either. We didn't talk much. My grandfather enjoyed the wedding, the city, the time with the always-huge Scotchie clan, Buddy division (my father's Ohio nickname). Later, my father told me: "Do you know what your grandfather said: 'Why don't you buy them a house?'" So he was impressed. I said nothing. At the time, that gift wasn't necessary. But I would call my folks on that request (at least a downpayment) when the little ones arrived (as I had better for them, someday).

A CONFEDERACY OF UNCLES

Ohio, like Asheville, was the world of jockery. At that age, what else is there? Youngstown was also a confederacy of uncles. Uncle Jim, Bob's nearest older brother was an All-Star jock at Austintown Fitch in the early Sixties. Football, basketball, track. An AHS yearbook had a photo of him in action as a pole vaulter, Jim flying over the bar, the pole being flipped in another direction, That, to me, was amazing. The red and black (Fitch colors) pole was still in the huge (three big rooms) basement. I spent a summer in the backyard, practicing in vain to be Uncle Jim, while an occasional rummy looked on from the parking lot. These were baseball summers. My Uncle Tony (from the Bruno's side) and myself, plus Uncle Bob and myself played whiffle ball for hours on end, using a wooden bat. There was Tony's slow curve (he said he was "The Big Bear," Mike Garcia) and Bobby's nasty slider. My uncles liked all this. They were still childless and playing with their nephews let them be kids again. It's an easy relationship, uncle and nephew: You play ball, you wrestle, you go to ballgames. Advice here and there, but no great pressure.

As with grandparents, I had no favorites. But I was closest to Uncle Bob, who was the youngest of the six boys. He was a big man, 6'4" and he knew it, too. Bob was like an older brother to me. He was a rabid Browns fan who chose basketball as his sport. When I started Little League, he wished me luck in "Grapefruit League" and that meant something to me. He had his own jock story. Following in Jimmy's big footsteps, he played basketball at Austintown Fitch. Progress was slow. So, in the summer between his junior and senior year, he beefed up, worked out every day, determined to make his last year at Fitch a big one. And it was. He was a top scorer for the 1964 Austintown Fitch Falcons, earning a spot on the Mount Union College squad the next year. This, too, impressed me. I read the 1964 Fitch yearbook over and over again, soaking up the games where Bob scored big, 20 points or more. He read it, too. Once, years later, I found him dozing off from an afternoon nap, the '64 yearbook by his side, still open.

Bob was also the brother who stayed in Austintown. All of his siblings went to college or the service, wanting to get out of saloon life. Being the youngest, Bob might have felt an obligation to stay on and help his parents. He once complained to my wife and myself about the job. "It's not the most uplifting thing in the world," he confided. "Here you are filling one drink after another to someone already pretty wasted," he added with a smirk toward the memory. Alas, saloon life had its problems, which led to recoveries, which led to Bob finding fulfillment as a counselor. Most of all, there were the trips to mighty Municipal Stadium. Uncle Bob, myself and my younger brother would all drive up. Tom gave us plenty of laughs. Once we wanted hot dogs and soda from a vendor prowling the aisles. Bob yelled—the guy didn't hear. I yelled—no response. Finally, little Tom belted out, "Hey, BUDD—*eeee!*" It worked. The vendor turned around as if someone had shot a hot poker up his backside. On the way home, Bob got lost. We were driving down a dark, empty road. "Ya know where ya goin'?" I sheepishly piped up. Bob paused. "No!" he blurted out, laughing. We all joined in. Time. Who needs it? Bob would talk about his women problems. On he went. Grandma Scotchie didn't understand his hang-ups over this girl or that girl. Again, Tom spoke up. "Just tell, Grandma, 'Gee, Mom I got to have a *chance* in life!'" Bob howled on and on over that one. "Right. I'll tell Mom, 'Gee, mom, I got to have a *chance* in life.'" We all laughed on, driving lost and happy, down dark highways.

My uncles all liked the 61-mile drive to C-Town. It gave them a chance to get out of the house, to spend time with nephews who obviously idolized them, to spend a few relaxing hours in the spacious ballpark.

In 1967, Tony and I traveled to Municipal Stadium for the summer ritual. We bumped into Mickey Mantle before a Yankee-Tribe game. "There he is," Tony said, pointing to The Mick. "Say something to him." Tony was an Indians fan and could care less about the damn Yankees. Mantle was dressed to the nines: A blue blazer, blue trousers, white shirt, a blue necktie with a white "NY" emblazoned on it. A smiling Mantle strolled by the gawkers. The next year, my Uncle Irv took us to another Yankee-Tribe game. The Yanks had signed Andy Kosco, an outfielder who grew up with Youngstown and was friends with Irv. So my man Irv got Tom and myself right to the door of the Yankee clubhouse where I stared as dumbly as I did at Mantle (Kosco was *huge*), while Irv and Kosco exchanged pleasantries. And what a game! It was a doubleheader and as everyone assumed, Mantle's last year in the bigs and with it, his last appearance in Cleveland against a team he had tormented for years. Still, he got a nice hand each time up and then Luis Tiant, the Tribe hurler, went ahead and ruined the trip, whiffing Mickey three times in the first game, overhand fastball smoking. The rout was on. Rocky Colavito was ending his career with the hometown Yanks and the fans, who once worshipped Rocky, booed him too, taunting him as "clubfoot." Mickey was now being booed and even Kosco was being taunted as clubfoot. Irv, raised in Brooklyn's rough and tumble Bed-Sty neighborhood and a Merchant Marine to boot, gave those drunks a hard look. They were lucky. Irv could have handled them easily (it'd be ugly). (Once, we were at a red light in Youngstown. When it turned green, Irv apparently didn't move fast enough. The punk behind us, trying to impress his girl, gave Irv the finger. Bad move. "That's it!" he roared, slamming the door and nearly sending the light sedan over flat on its right side. "You damn hippie!" is all I remember Irv yelling at the young greaser who, too, got off easy. Irv was a gentleman through and through, his glare alone could shut people up.)

Yes, the world of uncles. Also the world of the late Forties. As soon as you pulled out of The Inn, you hit the interstate and the sign, "Cleveland: 60 miles." How wild was that? Well, the National Football League, from the late Forties to the mid-Sixties, had a protective policy: It would not allow the broadcast of any home football game within 60 miles of that town's limits. The Inn, then, was just over 60 miles from Cleveland. When the Browns had a big home game, the saloon was jammed with fans. I could imagine those halcyon days: The little black and white television perched on beer crates under the stuffed deer's head, blaring out the games, while Otto Graham, Dante Lavell, Marion Motley and Lou Groza ran rings around the opposition. Everyone in Ohio loved the Browns, the Bama of the Buckeye State. It was undoubtedly the only team to be named for its head coach, Paul Brown, a man as equally beloved in these parts as Bear Bryant was down South. People still talked about Brown's legendary career as a high school football coach in Massillon, 20,000 fans showing for the Ohio version of Friday Night Lights. In the packed saloon, drinks and hot dogs flowed freely, the menfolk enjoyed the day off from the mill, while their womenfolk drank coffee and gossiped, nursing their babies in public.

Yes, 61 miles to mighty Cleveland. In 1963, the Bombers easily ruled the American League. A bunch of us—my father, grandfather, and some bar buddies—made my first trip to a big league Friday night game and a day later, a Sunday afternoon double dip. The Mick was injured, but this was the lordly Yankees of Maris, Ford, Howard, Richardson, Kubek, Pepitone, Clete Boyer, Yogi, Marshall Bridges, and Hal Reniff. Just watching batting practice was a thrill enough. On Sunday, the ballpark was a sea of kids wearing plastic Yankee blue batting helmets. By the seventh inning of the second game, I mustered up the courage to ask my father if I, too, could join the batting helmet brigades. He said no, not wanting to have spoiled children. Still, I loved that old ballpark, wooden seats, steel beams and all. With The Tribe going nowhere, the place became a joke. "Mistake by the lake" my eye! It was a grand old park, very democratic, just like the majestic Yankee Stadium. Eighty thousand people could squeeze in for a Brownie game. For baseball, anyone could see a game for $2.50 (or less) a pop.

We continued to go to games into the early Seventies when there was no Mickey Mantle to draw crowds. The Stadium was mostly empty, the teams not so hot, but we still had fun. I suffered along with The Tribe, but more so with the Brownies. All throughout the postwar years, Municipal Stadium was packed with 80,000 fans per home game. In 1964, the Browns even won an NFL title. By the Eighties, the fans called themselves "The Dawgs," a rip off, I thought (probably wrongly), of the 1981 University of Georgia national championship squad. In 1987, the Browns lost their best chance to make it to the Super Bowl when Denver Bronco quarterback John Elway engineered a famous 87-yard fourth quarter drive. The next year, they lost to that same Bronco team, a potentially-winning fourth quarter drive ruined by a fumble.

By the Nineties, the Browns were in decline. The owner Art Modell claimed the team was losing millions, so he up and left for Baltimore. Cleveland later received a new Browns franchise, but it was never the same. In the mid-Nineties, Municipal Stadium went down, replaced by a bland, state-of-the-art affair. On the old ballpark's last day, Cleveland native Bob Hope showed up as part of the farewell ceremonies. All of this was done with humor: the dump by the lake, gone at last! I still didn't like the ridicule, remembering always that huge outdoor frame of the grinning Indian greeting fans as they arrived at the park. As with the old, old Yankee Stadium, mighty Municipal lives only in the recesses of memory. And as with Asheville's new Farmer's Market, I shan't go to their replacement joints.

Uncles had benefits. So did the chores. Farm work, in truth, was pretty mild. During the summer months, my mother would yell at us, "come out and pick!" (help your poor grandparents). But, ma, we're on *vacation*. I dodged the corn and pea-picking but didn't mind mowing those five acres on Grandpa Bruno's mini-tractor. At The Inn, there was more lawn work, but not nearly so spacious. Grandpa Scotchie had a very light red electronic mower that made it easy to push up and down that steep, steep hill in the backyard. We also did barroom work. In the winter, when we did go up, we emptied the bottle cap tray and smashed dozens of those empty liquor bottles against the rocks at the bottom of the trash can area. There was little work for the sanitation crews. My grandfather opted, instead, to burn the trash. Other work wasn't so much fun. During that wasted youth, I didn't know yet what kind of writer I'd become. My mother felt that my paternal grandmother, who bore and raised six sons, might better understand boys and their wasty ways. Part of that was mopping The Inn's floor every Sunday morning (we were now closed on the Sabbath). Sweep and mop it once. Mop it again, said Grandma S. What? I finished up and my grandmother told me to mop that barroom floor again. I slammed down the heavy steel mop. We fussed back and forth until, finally, my grandmother shut me up for good. "You do it," Grandma said firmly. "I don't like that way of behaving.'" Your own grandmother! Giving you the business! It was like Grandpa Scotchie giving me grief for not eating all of the cucumbers. I looked it over. It wasn't *that* big a floor. Plus, it wasn't like I had a hot date waiting for me. So I mopped that floor again and for the rest of my seven months at The Inn, I swept and mopped that floor once, then mopped it twice. I flashed back on my Uncle Jimmy doing the same years earlier, while Grandma S supervised. At the least, I could do the same. In time, Grandma S gave me those big, earthy, jolly Polish grins and laughs. It was worth it. Maybe the boy will make it, yet. Yes, I badly wanted my grandparents' approval (please your grandfolks, of all people).

PRUDENT LIVING

The Inn taught prudent living. It was, after all, life among the alkies. The Sixties' Inn catered to an older crowd, folks who had married, raised their children and now wanted to get out of the house. There were workingmen and widows, too. Alcoholics, I quickly learned, were *loud*. Once, in 1964, my father and myself were set to go to Boardman to watch Uncle Bob play in a big conference showdown. We needed directions. All the old biddies and alkies were yelling and arguing over what route to take. They wanted to be helpful, but I didn't know what to make of this *noise* over directions to a high school basketball game. (The game, by the way, was great. The Boardman gym was packed, cigarette smoke rising to the ceiling. At halftime, Bob's coach took him aside and gave him a good dressing down. Hey, my uncle! Leave 'em alone! Bob got the message. He later scored a big goal on an offensive rebound. "Hey, Bob!" my father roared, full-throated from the upper deck. They didn't see each other often. My father was born in 1931; Bob in 1946. That roar was brotherly love from across the years.)

In the Seventies, the clientele changed. The Sixties crowd grew infirm or died off. The Seventies folks were younger, twenty-somethings either married and without children yet or still single. In recessionary times, people were waiting longer for marriage and family. Uncle Bob and his pals loved to tell tall tales of the old days: Chickie and Marie, two old biddies, fighting and pulling each other's hair out in the parking lot, a female version of the scene in "A Boy Named Sue." I had friends from the Seventies days: One day, Mitch Lamppole and Henry Wazowski were in a fighting mood. Mitch, who was much bigger, pulled the seat from under Henry as he went to sit down. Henry, a little fighter, went after him. Too ugly to watch.

The barroom brawls were mostly comical. Once, some bearded dope in a black leather jacket started a fight. He felt he had been cheated in a pool game by a local hustler. The rumble broke out everywhere. My grandmother was incensed. Fights were bad for business. Grandma S whacked him good with a cue stick. "You son of a bitch! You son of a bitch!" My grandmother in a brawl! I jumped in, rolling around the checkered floor. What for? My grandmother continued to plummet the young punk. It was funny. A dude getting clocked by a 70-year-old grandma isn't much of a threat to anyone. Grandma S didn't need *my* help.

Not all incidents were so slapstick. The late Sixties, to reiterate, saw anarchy and violence nearly everywhere in the U.S. Little Austintown wasn't exempt. There may or may not have been burglary attempts at The Inn in the past, but in the insanity-has-prevailed summer of 1968, it happened. I overheard my relatives whispering the story: They claimed that three crooks—two men and one woman—dressed in masks tried to rob the cash register. Not enough dough for them. So they walked into the house where my grandfather was holding court, presiding over a meal with his Warren in-laws. One of the men put a shotgun to Grandpa S's head. "What's this?" my grandfather replied. "Halloween?" The crook turned and left, without the dough. They escaped back to Youngstown, where they ran into the city's finest. Was it true? At the time, Uncle Jim's wife was expecting the couple's first child. They were also scheduled to join the family for dinner. My family members fretted that the trauma of the event would have badly affected the pregnancy. I didn't see it that way. Jim, like Irv, was a bruiser, not a man to be trifled with. In my mind, he would have manhandled those ski mask robbers easily.

A mere adolescent, I was enormously impressed with my grandfather's courage. A new story to brag about. On the first day of school, we St. Eugene's students, like everyone else, told the usual what-I-did-with-my-summer tales. We'd trudge up to Mrs. Ledbettter's desk and brag. One fall, it went like this:

"We went to London and Paris this summer."

"You did?" Mrs. Ledbetter asked, eyes growing as big as walnuts.

"Yep," I replied, triumphantly adding, "London, Kentucky and Paris, Kentucky!"

Next fall, a different story.

"Three robbers in masks came into my grandfather's saloon," I started up. The teacher said nothing, so I plunged forward. "They went back into the house and one of them put a shotgun to my grandfather's head. You know what grandpa said?" I asked, finishing with a flourish. "What is this—Halloween?"

"He *did*?" Mrs. Ledbetter answered, eyes still large, no change at all from last year's expression. The teacher still had many more tales to hear. No need to get worked up over any of them.

I won't exaggerate. The Inn was hardly a crime's nest, even though poor old Youngstown would disintegrate badly in the years to come. My grandparents loved The Inn. They could never sell it for, say, a nice, two-bedroom apartment. My grandfather whistled to work each morning, neatly buttoning up the blue work shirt with The Seven Mile Inn logo. For years, The Inn had a crackerjack bowling team that filled the back of the bar with one king-sized trophy after another. In 1969, my grandfather had a mild stroke. The family humor remained intact. In Asheville, we were all nervous. However, when my father called him at the hospital, Pop was all jokes. "Hey, what's the matter with you, young fellow?" My father roared with delight. "You're not supposed to get sick!" My grandfather easily recovered. He lived another 20 years, but he never bowled again and this bothered him tremendously. He'd sit at the back room table, watching television and squeezing a hand grip hours on end, trying to get back the magic. My grandmother loved the place, too. It was home. Every night, Grandma S held court near the back table, entertaining generations of customers, making sure the food and drinks were fine, talking gossip, family life and politics.

Summers ended in a flash. My father would drive up, unannounced and get us packing back to Asheville the next day. No one liked it, we all wanted to stay longer. But fall—and school—beckoned. My mother had anxieties, too. Goodbyes were long and tearful. One summer, it got to be too much. Tom loved the Bruno's five acres. He was a grade schooler, but they allowed him to ride on that tractor all day long. That he did, with a satisfied smile on his face as he felt all grown up and responsible. He had a friend next door, Dean, to play with. He loved the farm, helping his grandparents with goat's milk, the planting, even with homemade *vino*. He hated to leave—with two weeks of summer left at that. Again, it was too much. Tom was crying. My mother and my siblings were crying. "Honey, can't you do *some*thing?" my mother pleaded. "They don't have school for two weeks." My father said nothing. He flicked on the turn signal, pulled right into a private driveway, backed up when the coast was clear and made a beeline to 1691 Canfield-Niles Road, where my grandparents were waiting. They were delighted to see Tom, big hugs all around. "I'll pick him up in two weeks," my father announced, stepping back into the car. We were all glad for Tom. It made sense. Give the boy some fun before school starts. Plus, we'd all have more leg room for the 12-hour trip back home. My father didn't mind. He liked long distance driving. It gave him time to take the short cut route through West Virginia and see the old homeplaces, while a Pirate game on the radio kept him company.

In time, my mother, as she once related, realized her life was back in Asheville with the family. My mother was the only one of her sisters to leave Ohio. It wasn't easy. In time, also, sadness. In 1984, my maternal grandmother passed away. There was a huge wake at the homestead. I flew in from New York as fast as possible. "You missed a great wake!" my father told me when I arrived. "So many, people. Joey, you wouldn't believe it." It was good, I think, for my father to relieve, for one night, the glorious, happy days of the late Forties. "Oh, honey," my mother protested. After all, I *had* hightailed it in.

The funeral was not in Austintown, but back in Oakland Heights, now a pretty empty neighborhood, an occasional one-story house among the weeds and tall grass. The family took it hard, tears flowing freely, my grandfather expressing his love to his wife in both English and Italian. This was the first death. Something else had happened in Youngstown. In the early Eighties, it produced a middleweight champ, the highly popular Ray "Boom Boom" Mancini. Whenever Ray won a fight on ESPN, he'd happily shout out: "And hel-lo to everyone in my hometown....*Youngs*town, O-hi-o!" The city needed that badly. My Aunt Rosemary had connections and Ray, at the peak of his fame, traveled to Austintown to console my grandfather.

The next deaths weren't so traumatic. My surviving grandparents made it to their late eighties and early nineties. Grandpa Scotchie died in 1989. Grandma S held fort at the saloon. Grandpa Bruno died in 1995, after seeing that one last cornfield growing on the five acres. Grandma Scotchie was the last survivor, dying in 1998. It wasn't easy, those final years. Youngstown was now in collapse, the mills down, the city de-populating, the Bloods and Crips moving in from the coast. Poor Grandma S lived in fear of crime. The local police told her not to worry. They constructed an elaborate alarm system inside The Inn. It worked. One late night, some punk tried breaking in. He heard the alarm, then turned tail and hauled his sorry carcass back to Youngstown. My grandmother's death was sad, but she had lived long enough to celebrate the 50th anniversary of The Inn and to receive a nice write-up in *The Youngstown Vindicator*. At the wake, the family was philosophical. It had been a good life. Uncle Bob said that he would keep The Inn in top shape, just as my grandmother would have wanted. Apparently, however, The Inn lost money under new management. Uncle Bob, now involved with his counseling business decided, along with Uncle Frank, to sell it.

Shortly thereafter, a cousin was getting married. We went to the wedding, but I was nervous that The Inn would have been sold by then. I had heard the rumors. No last visit. From the Pittsburgh airport, we approached The Inn from North Jackson and Meander Lake. Hooray! The "7 Mile Inn" red light was on. Still open! My brother, his sons and myself steeled ourselves for one last weekend at

Our Favorite Place On Earth. In fact, the sale had been made; it was just a matter of months before the transaction was complete. And so, The Inn, in its final days, was packed by young people, younger than my brother or myself had ever seen. A karaoke competition was underway. On the blackboard behind the pool table, there was a chalk drawing of "Andy and Annie" with tears coming down on their cheeks. My grandparents! My grandfather had been dead for nine years. Now, it was like he was still alive. It was tough on my brother and myself. We walked into the packed joint and *nobody* knew us—-didn't know we were Scotchies! Fortunately, the barmaid was understanding. I told stories about scarfing down those broiled hot dogs, drinking Seven-Ups, playing pool and pinball, watching The Tribe with the Old Man, being placed on the barroom stool when I was a toddler. The barmaid let me work/hang out behind the bar. I scarfed down the final hot dogs and washed dirty glasses for her. By gosh, there was an old timer to my right, at the end of the bar, having a smoke, nursing a mixed drink, staring ahead. He looked like Grandpa Scotchie. Well, not exactly, a few years younger than I remembered the Old Man, but behaving the same: Quiet, stoic, deep in thought. All this, I was positive, was serendipitous. I didn't say a word to the old timer. Just took it all in and contemplated my good luck at seeing The Inn one last time.

VII.

WHAT ARE WE FIGHTING FOR?

1965: A PRELUDE

Happy America, you say? Sure, early Sixties folk had the chance to live normal lives: Jobs that paid, jobs with Christmas bonuses, marriage, down payment, two or three or more children. It all turned into Unhappy, if not downright Ugly America. November 22, 1963 was the traumatic date. Nineteen sixty-five was the tipping point. What happened since then was a free fall: The times turned into a roller coaster ride with the brakes off. A few analogies. Dies the literature, dies the nation? The two great novelists of the modern era—Ernest Hemingway and William Faulkner and the two great poets, Robert Frost and T.S. Eliot—all died before the fan hit the gluepot: Hemingway in 1961 of a suicide (initially reported as a gun-cleaning accident), Faulkner in 1962 (succumbing on the heels of an unfortunate binge, age 65, not "old" now, but considered so then), the great Frost in 1963 (he lived into his ninth decade and recited, from memory, his immortal "The Gift Outright" at the Kennedy inaugural) and finally, the master of modernism, T.S. Eliot, in January 1965, by then a longtime British subject living in London.

All of these men were down on the American prospect. Hemingway was at his happiest while living, first, in Paris, then in Cuba. After seeing the horrors of war in Europe, he was disgusted by the frivolity of life in his native Midwest: so back to Paris and *The Sun Also Rises*. Faulkner and Frost were both wedded to the land. There was Faulkner's hundreds of acres in Oxford and later, Charlottesville, while Frost, at one time, owned no less than five farms in his beloved New Hampshire. Faulkner was obsessed with the nobility of the Old South. Frost, a copperhead, sympathized with the South's plight throughout its tortured history. Eliot, as noted, was a British subject, a royalist and Anglo-Catholic who believed that American civilization had hit the skids with the election of Andrew Jackson in 1832 and the coming of mass democracy. The postwar era had its greats: Bellow, Updike, Tom Wolfe, Wendell Berry, Robert Lowell, James Dickey. Was it the same? On his television show, Charlie Rose once asked John Updike about the continuing appeal of both Hemingway and Faulkner. Updike responded that such men wrote with an intensity that still shone brightly, implying that such passion was lacking in the post-1945 world.

The other analogy? The fall of the mighty Yankees. (Here I am influenced by a Donald Kagan essay in David Brooks' *Onward and Upward*. The end of the Yankee dynasty, the end of content America.) From 1921-1964, the Yankees ruled. Every fall, a packed Yankee Stadium, complete with World Series bunting, was the essence of America, symbolizing American excellence, American continuity, American grace and style, American tradition. The Yankees were the face of the American Century: Efficient, poised, professional, stoic; quiet winners who did not gloat while winning one World Series after another. They were a colorful team with a flair for the dramatic. Yes, there was the Yankees of Babe Ruth, Lou Gehrig and Joe DiMaggio that plummeted the opposition, but also the Bombers of the Fifties, who weren't always the best team, defeating the Brooklyn Dodger powerhouse, prevailing over the Ted Williams Red Sox, plus the Cleveland Indians, a team with no less than three Hall of Famers in the starting rotation (Bob Lemon, Early Wynn, and the aging Bob Feller).

The Yankees, too, were an amalgamation of that 1910s to 1960s America: Old stock (Jack Chesbro, Frank Baker, Miller Higgins), Ellis Island (Gehrig, DiMaggio, Frank Crosetti, Tony

Lazzeri, Phil Rizzuto, Yogi Berra, Gil McDougal, Eddie Lopat), city boys (Whitey Ford and Billy Martin), country boys (Earle Combs, Bill Dickey, Enos Slaughter), stolid Midwesterners (Waite Hoyt, Tommy Henrich, Hank Bauer, Gene Woodling, Elston Howard, Tony Kubek). The Fifties' Yankees were led by Casey Stengel and Mickey Mantle. "Casey." "Mickey." You can't find two names more American. Injuries, old age, the refusal to sign such local talent as Rocky Colavito and Carl Yastrzemski to bonus contracts and the ill-advised firing of baseball's greatest general manager, George Weiss, also conspired to bring the Yankees down. It was shocking, these changes. The deaths of Hemingway, Faulkner, Frost and Eliot, the 1965 immigration bill and the end of Eurocentric America. The fall of the Yankees was even more dramatic: The annual autumn ritual of a packed Yankee Stadium gave way to the shock of 1965 and 1966: An empty stadium, last place teams, Mantle hobbling around the outfield on one leg. And more: The unraveling of the once-bustling The Bronx, once-mighty New York City, supremely confident America. Years later, when my mother-in-law battled seniority, the son-in-law had the right medicine: Bring up the old Yankees! The old New York. Just say the magic names, "Joe DiMaggio," "Yogi Berra," "Phil Rizzuto." It worked. Mother-in-law would light up, decades vanishing in front of the eyes. "Oh, yes! Joe DiMaggio!" Exactly. DiMag. Yogi. The Scooter. When real men walked the streets of Gotham, real gentlemen dressed in suits, ties and fedoras, no matter what their station in life was. Real men who opened doors for the ladies. A city where no punk would dare commit crimes against the elderly. The nation seemed lost, hopelessly so, without those fall afternoons in The Bronx.

THE BIG FOOL SAYS CARRY ON

Above all, 1965 America meant Vietnam. Lyndon Johnson, flush from a 44-state landslide victory in 1964, declared nothing less than a Second Coming. Good enough. Then then he upped the troops total in South Vietnam from 5,000 advisors to 118,000 troops in 1965 alone, eventually reaching 500,000 by 1968. If not for Vietnam, the Sixties would not have turned out so ugly. If might not have been

America, circa 1940, but the decade wouldn't have been "the Sixties," either. Enjoying peace and prosperity, the nation's rulers, with some wisdom, might have concentrated on domestic issues. Ending the Cold War, the unfinished business of the Eisenhower years, might have took place.

It didn't happen. The Sixties meant Vietnam and 'Nam meant Lyndon Johnson. Forget the sentimental tears over the Kennedy brothers and Dr. King. The 1960s was LBJ's, all the way. Talk about being careful of what you wish for! Has that Chinese proverb applied more to any man than Lyndon Johnson? As a young man working on a public works project, Johnson dropped his shovel and shouted out: "Someday, I'm going to be president!" His life (the man was the son of a modest, but popular Texas state legislator) was aimed at that one goal. As a congressman, Johnson said or did little to imperil his image. In 1940, when the Texas delegation rallied behind native son Vice President John Garner's doomed challenge to President Roosevelt, Johnson read the tea leaves and refused to endorse Garner. The FDR brain trust remembered that favorably. After being out-cheated by then-Gov. Pappy O'Daniel in the 1940 senate race, Johnson, in 1948, made sure he would sew up the necessary votes in San Antonio and South Texas to win that year's barn burner. Once elected, Johnson gave a fiery speech opposing proposed civil rights legislation. That and other gestures put him on the good side of Sen. Richard Russell (D—GA), the leader of the Southern bloc and a man who used his clout to make Johnson that body's Majority Leader. In that position, Johnson became a national Democrat: He supported raises in Social Security payments, plus the first civil rights bill to pass since Reconstruction. It didn't work. Two failed presidential races followed. In 1960, however, he had made it to the national ticket as JFK's running mate. The boyhood dream came true in most tragic fashion. After the 1964 landslide, Johnson, as noted, upped the stakes in Vietnam. The man couldn't stand to lose a war. How would America look in the eyes of the world?

That "bitch of a war" did Johnson in. There was guns and butter, a tax surcharge, inflation (and to be fair, a balanced budget (but only briefly) in 1967). Most of all, violence abroad, violence at home.

There was the rioting of the Sixties and Seventies. Also, after Richard Nixon's election to the presidency, terrorism at home, the desire of militant, middle-class and upper-class college youth to "bring the war home." That they did. Random terrorism took place all across America, at an ROTC center in Colorado, at a National Guard armory in Wisconsin, a shopping mall in Pittsburgh, a selective service office in New York City, at the Pentagon in Washington, all culminating with the infamous bombing of a Manhattan townhouse by the Weatherman terror group. (They were making a bomb that went off accidently.)

Even we grade schoolers had a Vietnam moment. Our St. Eugene's Pony team was assigned a coach, Ted Hanson. He was a junior at then-Jerome Pressley, a thin, wiry guy, not much taller than us, with a crew cut. He wanted to be a good coach. We wanted to be good players. At first, practices were gung-ho, but we kept losing on Saturday. We lost and lost and by mid-season, we were bushed. At practice, we were getting lazier and lazier: Why bust it out, we thought? The public school boys were going to whip us good. Hanson noticed this. One day at practice, he gathered us around for a pep talk.

"Boys," he said. "I am sad. I don't like what I'm seeing. You're goofin' off, not trying, you think you're going to lose every Saturday." He got more emotional. "Boys. I don't have to do this. I could be at home, listening to The Beatles, playing my guitar, watching TV with my girlfriend." We snickered, but I thought: Yeah, the guy *is* in high school, guess he *does* have a girl. Hanson went on. "But, no, I'm here with you boys, teaching you how to play football, how to be good athletes, good sports." Choked up by his little speech, Hanson stopped. He didn't mention winning. It was the effort that counted. And it worked. We all clapped hands, broke up and went back to practice. We also started winning a few games. Football was fun again.

Hanson drove a Volkswagen bug from Pressley to practice. One day, he must have gotten some news from home. He left practice right away, ran across Culvern Street, jumped into the VW and sped off. What was that all about? He looked concerned, as if something urgent had happened. The next morning, *The Asheville Citizen* was on the kitchen table. Below the fold, on the left hand corner, there it was. The headline read:

COL. HANSON,

ASHEVILLE NATIVE,

DIES IN COMBAT

Accompanying it was a photo of the now-deceased soldier, dressed in full United States Marine uniform, American flag in the background. That was it. We were only boys, not understanding at all of the world and its misery. None of us talked about it at school or practice. The enormity of our coach, dedicated to these football-challenged boys, losing a brother in far-off Vietnam, was too much to bear. Coach Hanson was too overwhelmed by the loss to take up the now insignificant coaching job. There were his parents to think about. Plus, this high school lad would now have to face life without a beloved older brother. We got a new coach, Mike Barnes. When Barnes was a cop, he always came by Burger Heaven with that big pistol bulging out of his belt. Curtis treated him right. He dated one of our teammate's older sisters, more cause for adolescent joking. He helped us get over Coach Hanson. It was sad. We were grade schoolers. We forgot. And we never saw Coach Hanson again after that traumatic day.

As the mid-Sixties gave way to the late Sixties, the war was now everywhere. During dinner, my folks liked to watch the evening news. One night, General Westmoreland was on, an interview from the front. He was pretty upbeat, but his inoculator kept pressing him for an end-date. "General," asked either Huntley or Brinkley. "When is the war going to end? Three months? Six months?" The general evaded the question and kept up with his cautiously upbeat reports. Even a grade-schooler knew this was going to be a long war. The general couldn't answer! And this was America, a country that goes to war and *wins* its wars, usually in short order. Bad news. At school, the fellows talked about it at lunch. Larry Sanders expressed the prevailing view when he said that draft dodgers were "chicken—-." So how are we going to win? "Just bomb 'em!" Larry blurted out. Yeah, end the damn thing. "But what about all those innocent people?" a classmate piped up. Good question, images of defenseless, little Vietnamese flashing in our Catholic school-trained minds. "Well," Larry recovered. "Just say, 'all you innocent people move out of the way! Here comes the bombs!'" Everybody laughed. Vietnam was a problem for adults, such as they were.

Were my parents for or against the war? Children of World War II, they considered military duty a solemn honor. Right or wrong, you fight for your country. One night at the dinner table, my father put down the knife and fork and blurted out, "I think I'll go to Vietnam for a year. What do you say?" I felt proud. My father at war. Plus, it was only for one year. What could go wrong? My father was in his late 30s, too old for combat. I figured they'd give him a desk job and that would be that. He didn't go, of course. That was 1966, when the war seemed winnable. Their views changed. Was it because Vietnam went from a Kennedy/Johnson Democratic war to a Nixon/Kissinger Republican one? By 1968, the country had turned against the war. Just bring 'em home. Then came the June 27, 1969 issue of *Life*. That was the turning point in our household. Who can forget it? It was the most poignant issue any periodical has ever published. And it came in *Life*, the picture-prose chronicler of the American Century, a publication with a jaw-dropping circulation of 12 million in its peak years. The issue listed the photographs of the week's dead in Vietnam. On the cover was a sandy-haired young man. He looked like Winnie Cooper's older brother from *The Wonder Years* who, on the show, also died in the war. But this was real life. And that week—and many more afterwards, William C. Gearing, Jr. of Rochester, New York was the face of America. On the inside, was page after page of the week's dead. It was like looking at a high school yearbook, only these were faces of fallen warriors. Those guys had guts. It was more than that. You saw the fellows you grew up with, played ball with, went to school with, double-dated with; fellows who were bagging groceries at the local supermarket one moment, then off to Vietnam the next. It took 12 years for the follow-up. By the early Eighties, a number of Vietnam-era songs had come out, among them, tunes by Charlie Daniels and John Fogarty, but the sequel to the *Life* issue was Billy Joel's "Goodnight Saigon," especially the lyrics:

> Remember Charlie,
>
> Remember Baker,
>
> They left their childhood
>
> On every acre

That was Hanson. That was the fellows in *Life*. That was 58,000 Americans more. The number, 58,000. It was cemented in everyone's mind.

"If they ran an issue like that every week, the war would come to an end right away," my father declared in an after church conversation. So they were against it. In truth, by the time of that famous *Life* issue, the war was winding down. In 1965, Rolling Thunder took off. The next year, the Democrats took a hit at the polls, losing 47 seats in the House of Representatives. Nineteen sixty-seven saw the big march on the Pentagon, dramatized in Mailer's *Armies Of The Night*. Finally, in 1968, Eugene McCarthy challenged Lyndon Johnson in that year's New Hampshire presidential primary, stunning the unsuspecting president by scoring 42 percent of the vote and forcing LBJ out the presidential race altogether. That year, Richard Nixon had his "secret plan" to end the war, while Hubert Humphrey, his rival for the presidency, promised to halt Johnson's bombing policy in North Vietnam. Once elected, Nixon and Henry Kissinger began a steady troop withdrawal from Vietnam. After winning re-election in 1972, Nixon bombed the Hanoi harbors with a heavy arsenal of B-52s. Critics denounced the action as barbarism. Some of the war's supporters however, felt that such action should have taken place years earlier in, say, 1965. The average Joe no longer cared. He was just glad the war was over.

What were we fighting for? And, in the long run, did it matter? It all began in the mid-Fifties. After World War II, the great European empires were shutting down. That included the French holdings in Indochina. The world, too, was now American. The U.S. moved in, with the administration of Dwight D. Eisenhower vowing to prevent a takeover of South Vietnam from the communist/nationalist North Vietnam. Eisenhower gave guarantees. Kennedy and Johnson followed up on them. Kennedy sent in the advisors, Johnson the hundreds of thousands of troops. Cold War paranoia played a huge role. By the Fifties, the Red Scare was in full swing. Both Russia and China had the bomb. Half the world was communist. American schoolchildren practiced "duck and cover" routines under their desks. The "who lost China?" debate fueled Senator Joe McCarthy's red hunt. Defense Department officials such as Walt Whitman Rostow were afraid that if South Vietnam fell, a "who lost Vietnam?" and another round of McCarthyism was in the offing. Neither JFK nor LBJ wanted that. Plus, both men were fierce anticommunists when the majority of Democrats were just that, too. Both men took pride in America's overwhelming military superiority over Russia and China. Did the Bay of Pigs failure influence JFK? In the early Sixties, Robert F. Kennedy traveled to South Vietnam, giving a rip-roaring speech, declaring that what happened in Cuba would not be repeated in Vietnam. Mostly, it was a matter of dominos. LBJ once told Ferdinand Marcos that the reason we were in Vietnam was to insure that the Philippines, once American territory and home to the Clark and Subic military bases, would never fall to communist guerillas. Johnson was as serious as a heart attack on the subject. As John Lewis Gaddis wrote on his standard history of the Cold War, *Strategies of Containment*, LBJ saw a world gone under if America lost in Vietnam. "To leave Viet-Nam to its fate would shake... confidence...in the value of an American commitment and in the value of America's word," Johnson proclaimed in April 1965. And again, in May: "There are a hundred other little nations...watching what happens...If South Viet-Nam can be gobbled up, the same thing can happen to them."

Count 'em. One hundred countries! All in danger of going red. The Soviets could hardly sustain such an empire. Plus, LBJ underestimated the staying power of military regimes designed to keep such commies at bay.

As it turned out, Watergate was the turning point. By the early Seventies, the war was over, America had seemingly won. The boys were home and South Vietnam was holding off the North. The cover-up of the "third rate" burglary forced Nixon to resign. Mightily empowered, the Democratic Congress cut off all aid to South Vietnam. The rout was on. Nixon's successor, Gerald Ford, vainly reminded Congress of their obligations to Saigon, but Ford or, should we say, South Vietnam—never had a chance. Saigon fell in May 1975. Despair and cynicism was in the air. America actually losing a war. It didn't seem real. Still, even Ford seemed relieved that American involvement in Indochina was over for good.

Yes, dominos fell, most of them didn't. Vietnam, Laos, and Cambodia went totalitarian. It was ugly, millions killed in Pol Pot's war on his own people. Americans had to endure endless waves of boat people from all three now-failed states. In time, the communists fought amongst each other. In 1978, Vietnam invaded Cambodia. In 1979, China invaded Vietnam. All throughout the Seventies and Eighties, Vietnam did battle with Hmong rebels in Laos. Was all this over communism or just self-defense? Vietnam, for instance, claimed it went into Cambodia to beat back border skirmishes by the latter nation's notorious Khmer Rouge regime. The Seventies were also a heady time of détente: Nixon to China, Nixon to Russia, arms control, U.S.—U.S.S.R. cooperation in space. In 1975, the Helsinki accords got the body politic a little pregnant with human rights. Two years after Helsinki, Vaclav Havel and his Czech colleagues formed Charter 77, the first stirrings of freedom in that nation since the Prague spring. In 1980, Poland's *Solidamosc* made its debut. The Cold War was ending. When Jimmy Carter scolded American policy makers for their "inordinate fear of communism," he was ridiculed, but not entirely wrong. Following Vietnam, nations other than this Asian trio fell to the Soviets. But not 100! And not The Philippines, either. In the early Eighties, Soviet communism had peaked.

Outside of the eastern bloc and Cambodia, Laos, Vietnam and Afghanistan in Asia, there was Angola, Ethiopia and Mozambique in Africa, plus Cuba, Nicaragua and Grenada in Central America and the Caribbean. All poor, backward nations, none of them, when sufficiently countered, posing any threat to anyone, except their own hapless subjects. In 1985, Richard Nixon wrote a fine essay in *National Review* basically telling conservatives to calm down. All of the world's wealthy nations, those in Europe and Asia, were aligned against the Soviet Union. How bad was it? In his memoir of the 1968 presidential campaign, Pat Buchanan recalled a 1966 trip to Africa with then-private citizen Nixon. The old Ethiopian, Halie Selassie, assured his American guests that the spirituality of the African people would prevent a godless ideology like Marxist-Leninism from ever gaining traction on that continent. Which was true.

The postwar generations were children of the Cold War. Both parties, for decades, made sure their presidential nominees were veterans. Our world was defined by those heady summit meetings between the American president and the Soviet secretary general, two men deciding the fate of the planet. In time, I was strongly influenced by the John Lukacs analysis of the Cold War, namely that it should have all ended by the late Fifties. The Soviets, Lukacs claimed, wanted their sphere, but they also acted in a defensive manner. They allowed for a neutral Finland, a neutral Austria and an independent Yugoslavia. As early as 1952, the Soviets had to deal with an uprising in East Germany; plus, three years later, those in both Poland and Hungary. In 1952, a dying Joe Stalin offered a grand compromise: Unification of the two Germanys, a removal of all foreign troops from that country, along with an all-German army and free elections. Lukacs felt that outright rejection of this by both the Americans and the Germans was a mistake. James Burnham, the architect of the famed rollback policy, agreed that Nikita Khrushchev's famous 1956 speech denouncing Stalin-era crimes represented a real thaw, also. Eisenhower was succeeded by the idealistic John F. Kennedy, who promised to "bear any burden" (the U.S. had those kind of bucks) in the cause of liberty. With the

New Frontiersmen's failure to overthrow Castro at the Bay of Pigs, the building of the Berlin Wall, the eyeball-to-eyeball Cuban Missile Crisis and finally, Vietnam, the Cold War seemed to have a new life.

Supporters of American involvement in Vietnam weren't wrong. They long predicted a bloodbath if Americans yanked out too soon. Which, indeed, is what happened. And there was successful Soviet adventurism around the world, again prolonging the Cold War. At the same time, my friend Sam Francis had his own take on the disaster. The irrelevancy of American conservatism (a church I later joined), began with Vietnam. It was, after all, a liberal's war. Why should conservatives go along? As Thomas Woods III pointed out, the war was about more than stopping communism. It also was about creating a liberal, democratic society in South Vietnam, where none before had existed. The Great Society's pie in the sky also included an offer to the enemy, North Vietnam, to construct a Tennessee Valley Authority-style economic development program in the Mekong River.

And so, the Seventies saw the once staunchly anti-New Deal, anti-Great Society conservatives welcoming welfare-state liberals, the neoconservatives, into the fold. (At least they were anticommunist, the reasoning went.) The Eighties were Ronald Reagan's decade of peace and prosperity. The Nineties, however, saw George H.W. Bush launch America's first-ever Middle Eastern war, driving Iraq out of little Kuwait. The next decade saw the zenith of warmongering: The right's own liberal war, George W. Bush's 2003 invasion of Iraq, a war also for democracy. The once-America First GOP had now mimicked the Democrats, fighting wars for global perfection.

There were no antiwar protests in Asheville. The South, from the beginning, was instinctively anticommunist. A Christian people, they could not stomach a godless ideology—you couldn't even go to church on Sunday to hear the Good News! People would be lost, hopelessly so, in such a world.

Vietnam, like Korea, was not as popular as World War II. Like Korea, Vietnam was an undeclared war, which meant the American Congress and with it, the American people, were never all-out committed to these conflicts. The public grew tired of fighting without winning. Still, it didn't seem right to protest in public when the kid down the block was putting his neck on the line in a war few people understood.

Many Southern pols, considered among the most hawkish in the country, were skeptical over the conflict. A friend once told of a meeting he had with Mendel Rivers, a conservative congressman from Charleston. This friend, who matured into a prominent editor, expressed his doubts over the war. Rivers abruptly said that it was immoral to fight a war when you have no strategy of winning it. In his autobiography, Herman Talmadge, the equally conservative senator from Georgia, revealed his own misgivings. After the Bay of Pigs, the U.S., Talmadge acknowledged, needed to stand up to the Soviets somewhere in the world, but Vietnam wasn't the place (How quickly people forgot MacArthur's admonition against fighting Asian land wars!) Talmadge's legendary colleague from the Peach State, Richard Russell, held similar views.

Learning this years later surprised me. Few Southern pols were vocal in their opposition. Some were. In 1972, North Carolina's junior senator, Everett Jordan, attended an antiwar gathering that was deemed too leftist for the state's conservative voters who rejected him in his primary fight against a lawyer from Durham, Nick Galifinakis who in turn, lost the general election to Jesse Helms. The most intelligent opponent of the war was Arkansas senator, William J. Fulbright. A Rhodes Scholar, Fulbright became a media favorite for slamming the Johnson Administration's "arrogance of power." More important, Fulbright articulated a decent enough foreign policy for a nation suddenly thrust out of its traditional neutrality. The United States, Fulbright proclaimed, has no quarrel with the internal affairs of any country provided that nation has no designs upon America. LBJ couldn't stand Fulbright. He ridiculed the senator as "half bright" and soon withered from the heat of hearings that his fellow Dems were holding in the Senate. Fulbright was in the South's antiwar tradition of Henry "Light Horse Harry" Lee (opponent of the War of 1812), Jefferson Davis ("all we ask is to be left alone") and two Tar Heels: Claude Kitchen and Asheville's own Robert Reynolds. Kitchen, the House Majority Leader in 1917, opposed America's entry into World War I for the simple reason that Kaiser Wilhelm's Germany was not an enemy of the U.S. and posed no threat to America. Reynolds, a controversial character who grew up in downtown Asheville and briefly attended the University of North Carolina before embarking on a career of journalism, law, and politics, supported a strong defense in the face of German and Japanese imperialism. But he opposed American involvement in the European conflict, embittered by what he believed were British and French tactics to draw a reluctant public into more bloodletting. By 1944, Reynolds was so unpopular that he declined a re-election run.

Talmadge, Russell, Rivers, Fulbright, Kitchin, Reynolds. These long-forgotten pols were men I came later to admire, only after the much-ballouyed conservative movement and a squeamish Republican Party seemed incapable of arresting the nation's decline. My interest in their old-style fidelity to a constitutional republic took place long after the breed had passed from the American scene. Was the passing of the Southern Dems a good thing? Was it inevitable? The process had been in motion since the urban wing of the Democratic Party began to take charge in the 1920s. Meanwhile, the slam-bang events of the Sixties and Seventies would provide the dismal answer.

VIII.

You'd Have To Be From There

Normal America, yes; abnormal America, you bet! It wasn't until 1969 that I heard about a local teenage girl, all of 15, actually being pregnant and unmarried. Indeed, the world was coming to little Asheville. There, too, was sad America. Change was coming to the South. Everyone knew it. No one liked it. Old folks were sour. Even my friends, grade schoolers, hearing gloomy reports from around the dinner table, were irritable. If it's the South, then all roads lead to William Faulkner. "You wouldn't understand," the doomed Quentin Compson told his Canadian roommate at Harvard, Shreve McCaslin, in a dramatic scene from *Abaslom, Absalom!,* "you'd have to be from there." The upheavals of the Sixties and Seventies were something intimately felt by the Southern people. In the early Sixties, mid-South states like North Carolina would desegregate certain schools, while also having a school choice plan: Black students could attend white schools, whites could attend black schools. That achieved only partial desegregation. It wasn't good enough for the Supreme Court, by now the real rulers of America. Full desegregation came with complications: rioting, fights in hallways, the cafeteria, bathrooms, and smoking halls. It came with comity, also, the desire by those involved to make it work. There was voluntary desegregation (Little League, Y football) and now, the involuntary kind. In one instance, it seemed that there were more police at South French Broad than actual students. There were awkward moments, too. Once, in the mid-Seventies, after things had calmed down, we high schoolers took an end-of-the-year field trip to Carowinds in Charlotte. I hung out with a date and her girlfriend. On the way back, the bus stopped at a rest area outside Hickory. Five of us, four whites and a black, took advantage. An old timer came in. He was a little man, a ball cap on, wearing work clothes. He stopped and stared for a while. We didn't notice, washing up and drying off. The old timer spoke up. "What are you boys doing with him?" We all knew what he was talking about. We were stunned. No one could speak. Finally, Ken Clark, a class officer who became a physician in Nashville, spoke up. "He's a friend of ours," Ken affirmed. We all finished up and silently filed out.

Again, it was sad. The classmate, whose name I never knew, was a quiet fellow. Like Campbell, he was one of the 1,001 anonymous blokes who went through high school without being noticed by anyone. He was harmless. So too were us polite, middle-class boys. And so too was the old timer. He couldn't have meant it. Something else might have been bothering him.

I don't throw stones. Folks were embittered. A way of life, all that they had known, one that both the working and middle classes had sincerely believed made the best of a difficult situation (in the 1870s, educators who proposed a dual public school system for poor whites and blacks were considered the region's "first liberals"), all that was coming to an end—-and what replaced it was not necessarily going to be an improvement.

I was too young to understand all this. We didn't have roots in the region. Yes, our family had lived in West Virginia since the late nineteenth century, but the Mountaineer State held an entirely different set of dynamics. The South was being overwhelmed on all fronts. In the postwar era, America was thrust into a new world. The great European empires were shutting down. America was now charged with managing a bipolar world: Freedom (American-style democracy) vs. anti-imperialism (Soviet communism). And so, the franchise was at stake. To preach democracy abroad to the de-colonized world, America had to practice it fully at home. In fairness, this was a Deep South thing. After the war, the mid-South gradually granted universal enfranchisement (this included millions of whites who could never afford the poll tax). By the mid-Sixties, the only holdouts were a handful of counties in the Mississippi Delta and south Alabama, where white minorities tried to hang on to power. Back to Talmadge. "The 1965 bill was superfluous," the Georgian claimed in his autobiography. It was also punitive, placing eight Southern states under Federal election control. Public schools were a different matter. This represented the moment of truth. The poet Allen Tate suggested that the South be allowed to deal with the franchise before tackling the schools issue. Which never was going to happen. As Mark Royden Winchell, the literary essayist/biographer observed:

> The fight against industrialism had failed. Everywhere the Southern tradition was vilified. It there was one stand to be taken, it was against interference in the Southern community.

Here, the resistance wasn't wrong. The busing orders of the late Sixties and early Seventies turned into a monumental wipeout. Why? Well, once the orders were issued, the middle class, in short time, left such districts and often, entire cities. I'm no fan of public schools, but from my teaching experience, such factories can only work if they have a middle class base. With busing, thousands of school districts lost their middle class student bodies and with it, their middle class revenue base. Asheville and Buncombe County was not part of this nationwide collapse (one that will bedevil this nation for time immemorial). A blow, yes. Initially, black students were bussed crosstown to a North Asheville white elementary school. White students were bussed to a junior high school on Hill Street downtown. No one liked it. Both races were sour. They both were losing institutions they had each built up and nurtured over the past 90 years. Both Jerome Pressley and Robert Coalfield High Schools could boast of their own sports teams, bands, cheerleaders, majorettes, various academic clubs; big cases full of trophies in the main rotunda, not to mention illustrious graduates who had contributed to the world of business, medicine, education, politics, law, and theology. Decades and decades of hard work was going right down the tubes. One morning, my father was driving us to VHS. Two buses steamed in opposition directions. "That's the stupidest thing I ever saw," my father said. "A bus?" I replied, playing dumb. Teenagers don't think about such things, the mind being on girls, cars, sports. (Plus, I didn't want to get into a fight over politics.) In 1972, North Carolina Democrats voted for George Wallace in the state's first-ever presidential primary. In 1980, my folks, who were with Jimmy Carter in 1976, voted this time for Ronald Reagan. And that's another story.

In the Seventies and beyond, much was made that desegregation worked better in the South than in Northern cities. Which was generally true. It was easier for desegregation to work in, say, Buncombe County than in New York or Boston. Buncombe County, outside of Asheville. The population shared the same Protestant religion, the same attachment to the land, a shared history. What did folks up North have in common? Here, Ellis Island students, two generations removed from the Old Country, were bunched in together with a black population now arriving from the rural South. I saw this upfront, too, from my adopted town, NYC. This was sheer cruelty, student abuse, American-style. I won't exaggerate. The situation in Southern cities like Atlanta and Birmingham, turned out no different than their Northern counterparts. So I contradict myself. In *I'll Take My Stand*, John Gould Fletcher fretted that public schools in the region, if centralized, would lose their local color, their diversity and "the charm of our South," resulting in a school system now "assimilated outwardly and inwardly to the street gangs of New York and Chicago." No kidding. Along the way, there was some levity involved. In 1974, Boston was riveted by a busing crisis that received national attention. In time, administrators from that city traveled to Charlotte to see how desegregation might work. Political cartoonists had fun with that. Look at who are the good boys now!

And so, the South was forced to walk the plank. For past sins. For moral reasons. For, even, geopolitical ones. Did it work? Yes, everyone involved—administrators, teachers, parents, students—

tried to make the best of a trying situation. In 1976, Jimmy Carter campaigned for president throughout the South, praising local schools for doing just that. Was learning compromised? Could the curriculum remain the same? How could one teach, say, Civil War history to an integrated classroom without feelings being bruised, students feeling slighted, even angry, causing trouble, making teaching impossible? Consult the 1993 National History Standards. No mention of Paul Revere, Patrick Henry, Thomas Edison, Booker T. Washington, Robert E. Lee, and Jonas Salk. Was that the result of social engineering? Or the rise of multiculturalism that came later in the Eighties?

Again, this wasn't true everywhere, not yet. The Sixties and Seventies America was still a Washington-Lincoln-Jefferson nation. Southern state capitols could still fly a Confederate flag. Confederate monuments were safe. At VHS, there were Latin Clubs, French Clubs, Spanish Clubs. The American literature courses taught the standards: Hemingway, Faulkner, Fitzgerald, Steinbeck, and Wolfe. I was too dreamy to take advantage of this, my mind being on the big city and what it might have to offer.

RFK

In 1968, things came to a head. The story of that year has been told countless times: The Viet Cong Tet offensive (an American victory, by the way) that advanced to the outskirts of Saigon, McCarthy's upset of LBJ in the New Hampshire primary, assassinations, riots in the cities, riots at the Democratic Party convention, riots at Columbia University, upheaval in Paris and Mexico City, the Soviet invasion of Czechoslovakia, the resurrection of Richard Nixon and in December, the orbiting of the moon by Apollo 10 astronauts. (Folks were sure glad to see that year come to an end.)

The changes from America 1964 to America 1968 continue to amaze. In 1964, Barry Goldwater's campaign ran a TV ad showing juveniles running wild in the streets. Goldwater was savaged as an extremist. By 1968, juveniles going berserk was now smack dab mainstream. No one was snickering anymore.

We remained a Kennedy household. When Robert F. Kennedy announced for the presidency, my folks seemed pleased. We had the television on in the living room and there was Kennedy, surrounded by his wife and their brood of 10 children, speaking in the Senate rotunda. We all watched, my father standing up, hoping to hear the right words. I didn't know that RFK was despised by many on the left. After all, it was Eugene McCarthy who had the wherewithal to take on a sitting president, a man who did not suffer political enemies lightly. Now, Kennedy looked to pick up the pieces left by New Hampshire. Bitterness between the Kennedy and McCarthy camps was intense. Either way, Kennedy won early primaries in Kansas, Nebraska, Indiana, and Wisconsin. It seemed natural to me. Kennedys don't lose elections. Then Kennedy went off to Oregon and lost the primary to the persistent McCarthy. It was the first time a Kennedy had lost an election—any election—since 1946, when Jack first ran for Congress. And so, Kennedy and McCarthy faced off, *mano o mano*, in the California primary. There, Kennedy won by a 46-42 percent margin. He gave a speech imploring his charges that it was "on to Chicago and let's win it there." Kennedy had admitted that "Daley is the ballgame," referring to Richard J., the kingmaker mayor of the Windy City, where the big convention would be held. Nineteen sixty-eight, in fact, was the last year when a politician could win the presidential nomination without entering a single primary. All they needed was support of labor bosses, governors, big city mayors (Democrats) or the Board of Directors of Chase Manhattan Bank (Republicans). Could Daley come through for Kennedy?

No one was surprised when they heard the news. It was almost expected. After Kennedy was shot, I remember learning that the "F" in his middle name stood for "Francis," not "Fitzgerald" that Jack Kennedy's was. School was out. There were no lawns to mow that June 5. It was just another day playing ball with my buddies in stay-at-home moms America. People kept hollering out the latest from Good Samaritan Hospital in Los Angeles, where Kennedy lay bedridden. All my friends and I could talk about was that Kennedy's two bodyguards—Rafer Johnson and Rosey Grier—had been jocks we watched on television: Johnson, the Olympiad, Grier, an All-Pro defensive tackle for the Los Angeles Rams. There was no Secret

Service detail for poor Kennedy. Neither Johnson nor Grier were qualified for such an enormous responsibility. Was the American government still that short sighted?

That was June 5, 1968. The next day, Kennedy perished. And so, another weekend of agony for a nation in mourning. My father and myself were laying down a new tile for the upstairs bathroom. On the box, the funeral train chugged through the countryside, from Washington to New York. You saw people clustered together, holding signs and weeping. You saw a sole mourner running after the train at full speed. The poor of America, white and black, had crowded the lost byways to greet the funeral train. On board, Kennedy's eldest son, Robert Jr., then 14, dressed in a suit and tie, walked from car to car, shaking hands and greeting the mourners, putting on a brave face similar to John-John's salute of his father's casket. "He's got it. The boy's got it," Ethel Kennedy reportedly told friends. I didn't want to watch anymore. Get this over with. "Hey, Dad," I piped up. "Ready to lay down more tile?" I thought that my father would be pleased: A son who'd rather work than watch television. I was wrong.

"Can't you see what's happening?" my father sputtered, motioning toward the box. He wanted to say more but couldn't. The funeral was similar to that of the slain senator's older brother. America, 1968, still dressed for the occasion: Men in suits, ties and polished shoes, ladies in dresses, gloves, and high heels. The funeral at St. Patrick's ended with Ted Kennedy's eulogy. "Some men see things as they are and say why. I dream things that never were and say why not," the senator concluded, quoting his slain brother. I did not know until much later that Ted Kennedy was closer to RFK than the president, always revealing a more human side, lightening up significantly when talking about "Bob" and his youthful exploits. Even as a famous politician, Ted Kennedy clearly looked up to his older brother.

After Kennedy's death, my mother decided to give McCarthy a look. We went to McCarthy headquarters on Merrimon Avenue and browsed. I read a paper describing how McCarthy could yet grab the nomination from Vice President Hubert Humphrey. (It wasn't very convincing.) My mother bought a little McCarthy button and pinned it on my youngest sister. "Maybe they'll put you in the paper," my mother said as a way of convincing little Jennifer to be enlisted in a political campaign. That didn't happen, either. To the South, McCarthy was an alien as Kennedy. Once, McCarthy landed in Charlotte for a campaign stop and cheerfully announced, "it's great to be in South Carolina!" Years hence, liberals treated McCarthy as a dull yesteryear, while conservatives enjoyed mocking his supposedly flaky ways, such as writing poetry on the sly. It was a bum rap. By the time of McCarthy's passing in 2004, the senator's steadfast supporters had been Old Right types who admired McCarthy's antiwar views, plus his restrictionist stand on immigration. Iconoclastic as ever, McCarthy had publicly regretted his vote for the 1965 Immigration Bill and America's ensuing disappearance as now "a colony of the world." When he ran as an ineffective third party candidate in the 1976 presidential race, the great Old Right traditionalist Russell Kirk stood by his old friend.

Kennedy died in June. In August, he made a reappearance on screen, at the Democratic Party convention. Wherever you went that summer, folks had the television tuned on to both conventions, probably the first and last time that this has happened. America, 1968, was a broken civilization, everyone knew it, but how in God's name could these get-along-go-along pols hope to fix the cracked vessel? In the early Sixties, Americans still had faith in their government to do the right thing. Highway construction, for instance, would be accompanied by a cheerful sign, "your tax dollars at work!" By the Seventies, cynicism had prevailed.

At the convention, there was a memorial documentary on Kennedy's life. There was Kennedy, just a few short months earlier, on the campaign trail, Beatles-style haircut waving in the wind, tie loosened, shirt sleeves rolled up, a healthy grin on his face as he campaigned from an open car, grasping the multitude of hands below. The background music played Peter, Paul and Mary's "If I Had A Hammer." And indeed, at that moment, it all seemed possible. The young Kennedy could hammer out "justice, freedom" and "love between my brothers and my sisters" all over this land. I looked around the den. My mother, my sisters, my brother all crying. The song went on, the crying in full force, unashamed, cathartic. Join them? No. My father was the only one not in the room. He was in the basement, tooling around, too disgusted to watch. So be the man of the house. My family members weren't the only ones. Disillusioned Kennedyites in the convention hall had seen an antiwar plank defeated and soon, Humphrey nominated. The film was cathartic for them, too. Or as Mailer observed in his minor classic, *Miami And The Siege Of Chicago*:

> The movie came to an end. Even dead, and on film, he was better and more moving than anything which had happened in their convention, and people were crying. An ovation began...Minutes went by and the ovation continued. People stood on their chairs and clapped their hands. Cries broke out. Signs were lifted. Small hand-lettered signs which read, "Bobby, Be With Us," and one enormous sign eight feet high, sorrowful as the rue in the throat—"Bobby, We Miss You," it said.

Nineteen sixty-eight was, I believe, the zenith of our family's admiration for the Kennedys. Concerning Edward Kennedy, it wasn't, as noted, Chappaquiddick that did it as much as rumors of philandering and his eventual divorce from his first wife, Joan, who had come down with a much-publicized drinking problem. Robert Kennedy had his older brother's charisma, the same promise of a better world. Still, consider the canyon of differences between the two men. They reflected the hard left turn the Democratic Party– and America–was taking as the Sixties progressed. JFK was a fierce anticommunist who authorized a failed invasion of Cuba, sent advisors to Vietnam and blockaded that same Cuba from a Soviet flotilla. RFK, in time, became an opponent of the Vietnam War and delivered no rhetorical broadsides against international communism. JFK's administration enacted the first across-the-board tax cuts since the conservative Calvin Coolidge. There was, again, the nomination of the pro-life Democrat, Bryon White, to the Supreme Court. JFK's response to poverty was the belief that "a rising tide lifts all boats." RFK signed up for a War on Poverty and did not view spending programs as especially detrimental. (He did call for civil rights to be accompanied by civic responsibility.) JFK only reluctantly supported federal civil rights legislation. He tried calling off Martin Luther King, Jr.'s 1963 March on Washington and as a native of Massachusetts, JFK was most sensitive about preventing the Democratic Solid South from turning Republican on his watch. In 1968, RFK, as far as I know, didn't even bother campaigning in the region. I won't exaggerate. Both men, especially JFK, supported a radical makeover of America through new immigration laws. The future brought busing, quotas, affirmative action, abortion, nationalized health care, gay rights. Where would the brothers have stood? Can't say, but I believe that RFK would have been more accommodating towards the Dems (and America's) never-ending leftward march.

THE ONE THAT GOT AWAY

Now to the other end of the spectrum. (It was that kind of year.) Kennedy, charismatic as he was, had no traction in the South. Sure, we Catholics claimed him, but he probably wasn't going to defeat Humphrey at Chicago and if he did, he wouldn't have won any Electoral College votes in the region. Someone else was gaining traction. By the late Sixties, George Wallace had replaced Strom Thurmond as the topic of discussion around the dinner table. The two were similar. Thurmond ran as a third party candidate in 1948, while Wallace did the same 20 years later. In the Fifties and Sixties, Thurmond was the leader of the Southern bloc in the U.S. Senate. He made the news, conducting a 20-hour filibuster against a 1957 civil rights bill, bolting the Democratic Party for the GOP in the Goldwater year of 1964, being a power broker at the 1968 GOP convention, securing delegates for Richard Nixon as the latter fended off a challenge from Ronald Reagan. In the mid-Sixties, Thurmond, now in his sixth decade, married a knockout blonde, a 20-something woman. That was a shocker alright. It reminded one of the photo of JFK coming out off the beach with a bevy of females around him.

Ninety sixty-eight was Wallace's year, too. The Wallace story, also, has been told numerous times: Rural middle-class upbringing in south Alabama, World War II service in the Air Force, a judgeship, a moderate who lost the 1958 governor's race to a segregationist leading to Wallace's conversion to that position by the time of his successful gubernatorial run in 1962. There was his brief run for the presidency in 1964, peaking at 21 percent in the polls in 1968, surviving an assassination attempt in 1972 before completing a full circle: Winning gubernatorial races in the Seventies and Eighties as a populist centrist, forging a biracial coalition that kept the rising Republican tide at bay. "I just hope the rich and powerful don't take over," Wallace reportedly said in January 1987, as he handed over the reins to the state's first Republican governor since Reconstruction.

The South was divided on Wallace. The Deep South liked his hell-for-leather style, one that ridiculed pointy-headed college professors who couldn't park their bicycles straight to the desire to take the briefcases from those meddling D.C. bureaucrats and chuck them into the Potomac River. That same style, however, did not play as well in genteel Virginia or bourgeois North Carolina. Plus, Wallace had running mate problems. His first choice was Happy Chandler, former governor of Kentucky. It made sense: A Deep South, Mid-South ticket. The only way for Wallace to have any impact was to win North Carolina, Tennessee, South Carolina, Kentucky, and Virginia, along with his Deep South base, denying, in the process, Nixon or Humphrey from earning the 270 electoral college votes needed for victory and throwing the election to the U.S. House of Representatives, where the Southern Democrat bloc would have some clout. However, Chandler, according to biographers, wasn't conservative enough when it came to civil rights issues. Such key Wallace donors as Lamar Hunt voiced their objections. Wallace, instead, choose Curtis LeMay, the hawkish former U.S. Air Force Chief of Staff, as his running mate. At the introductory press conference, Le May botched it badly, declaring that a nuclear exchange between any two countries would not result in the extermination of plant life or even animal species.

In October, Wallace held a rally at the City-County Plaza. My Uncle Jim, who was a political buff, took me along. It made sense for Wallace to come to the hub of Western North Carolina. He needed badly to win the state. In eastern North Carolina, Wallace ran strong, winning counties from the Virginia/North Carolina border down to the South Carolina state line. In fact, every county Wallace won in the eastern Carolina heartland had been taken eight years earlier by John F. Kennedy (you can look it up!). (It was that kind of decade.) However, Nixon was running strongly in both the Piedmont and in the mountains and Wallace needed to shore up support. It was a sunny, fall morning, the Columbus Day holiday. Wallace gave his stump speech. Most people cheered the applause lines, others stood with arms crossed. The crowd was mostly blue collar. Folks passed the hat for cash. Near the end, a heckler made the inevitable appearance. After an exchange, Wallace shot back, "And the truth is son, when this speech is over, come up here and I'll autograph your sandals!" Everyone roared, including us two skeptics. My teenage mind believed all this was a staged act that went from town to town. By the end of the speech, the folks who were on the fence clapped along with everyone else. Dollar bills went into the straw hats. "So," my uncle smiled as we drove home, "whaddya think?" Jimmy was amused, but not impressed with the political class of either party. "Ah, dunno," I blushed back. I thought of my friends at school, my parents. At our highly politicized parochial school (there was a war going on and us boys were reaching draft age), most of my classmate's parents were for Nixon, a chunk were for Humphrey, a lesser margin for Wallace (the students, naturally, followed their parents' sentiments). We did mock debates, where students, in pairs, made the case for either Nixon, Humphrey or Wallace. My friends were for Nixon and that influenced me, along with televised images of body bags and burning cities, all taking place under a Democratic administration. Still, I admired the Wallace classmates for sticking up for their man. We never talked about Wallace around the dinner table. Kennedy Democrats, my parents probably didn't care for the man, but being mindful of their neighbors and Southern custom, kept any negative thoughts to themselves. This still being a Democratic state, my mother commiserated with the kindly gas station attendant at the Merrimon Avenue Esso. He was a red-cheeked, sad-eyed man, a true yellow dog who wept at the news of Humphrey's defeat.

Running mate problems aside, Wallace was stymied by the new Nixon. The Nixon of 1968 was a radically different candidate from the vice president who lost a close (and possible illegal) election in 1960. Nixon now had a Southern strategy, he gunned hard for blue-collar ethnics in the Northeast and Midwest. It was Wallace who helped him become a changed man. Nixon talked tough on crime, welfare and busing. His campaign proclaimed the "civil right" of Americans to walk the streets of their cities without fear of violence. In the end, Nixon held off a hard-charging Humphrey, winning 32 states to Humphrey's 13 and Wallace's Deep South quintet. The popular vote was much closer, Nixon winning only by a 43-42 percent tally.

Wallace's third party challenge was the last one America would see until H. Ross Perot received 19 percent of the vote in 1992. In that time period, my reading habits had changed significantly, from fiction to non-fiction, the worldview of *National Review* and *The Wall Street Journal* editorial page to, finally, the Old Right of Patrick J. Buchanan and the scholars on the pages of *Chronicles*, among them M.E. Bradford and Clyde Wilson. In 1968, both Mel and Clyde supported Wallace. By the early Nineties, this influenced me significantly. For the Southland, a veritable font of literary genius, has not produced two more thorough and prolific scholars than either man. If Richard Weaver was the successor to Donald Davidson and Andrew Lytle, then Bradford was the successor to Weaver and Clyde the successor to Bradford. There was Bradford, the literary critic, prolific on Faulkner and the Agrarians, who was also America's greatest interpreter of the Declaration of Independence and the U.S. Constitution, explaining, in essay after essay, that both were deeply conservative documents seeking not upheaval, but to prevent the revolution against private property (and with it, English-style liberties) by King George III. And then his friend, Clyde Wilson, the polemical successor to Davidson, the world's leading authority on John C. Calhoun, the mirror image of Mel, an historian who also knew the Southern literary tradition backward and frontward, a man who better than anyone, explained the profound moral, religious and aesthetic differences between the puritan New England and the cavalier Southland. Both men, also, had deep roots in the region. Mel's ancestors helped to draft the post-Reconstruction Texas state constitution, while Clyde's were the last living Confederate veterans in North Carolina, an amazing achievement when one considers that the Tar Heel state had nine percent of the Confederacy's population, while providing 20 percent of the troops and suffering 25 percent of the casualties. For both, the South was a sacred trust. Both men of good will, neither could abide by such a social revolution. If Mel and Clyde were for Wallace, then that movement indeed had strong constitutional footing. Wallace's supporters had been ridiculed as much as the man himself: Backward bigots in pickup trucks. Mel and Clyde made the intellectual case for the Wallace candidacies and similar ones that followed. There was also my disillusionment with conservatism and the GOP (Clyde especially loathes the latter). I began voting for third party candidates: Perot, Pat Buchanan, other fellows whose names I couldn't even pronounce.

Wallace had his defects. His raw style scared off people and not just the middle class New South, but also Northern ethnics who eventually made their way back to Humphrey. Wallace had a moderate side, surprising Mike Wallace when he remarked in an interview that, if elected, he would "of course" include black Americans in his administration. No matter. In the Sixties, the South was under siege. Mark Winchell was right. The region was being vilified and ridiculed, savaged as knuckle-draggers in a nation devoted to Progress Unlimited. Also correct was Talmadge. Federal legislation did single out Southern states election districts and public school systems for an arbitrary—and punitive—takeover. The Southland needed to show the nation a united front, even in defeat. And if you think by now that the Mid South made a mistake by not joining the Deep South in voting for the Alabamian....well, you're getting warm. The summers of 1967 and 1968 represented two of the worst years in American history. In the fall of 1968, the American people had a chance to rectify the situation—and they blew it.

'68 MATTERS

Nineteen sixty-eight mattered. It represented the first electoral revolt against liberalism since 1932. Easy to see why. In front of your nose, as George Orwell might put it. On it went: 1972, 1980, 1984, 1988, 1994: Huge wins, election after election, for the "conservative" party. The Democratic Party victors of that era—Jimmy Carter and Bill Clinton—both emphasized their "moderate" roots. And, yet nothing happened. The Cold War was won, yes, but the culture war was a rout. The nation continued its sharp left turns: Not just abortion, busing, quotas, but now mass immigration, "hey, ho, Western civ has got to go" (multiculturalism). How'd it happen? Some history. My Old Right masters, Mel and Clyde among them, gloomily marked the Civil War as the end of republican governance and the triumph of a centralized regime. They have a point. America made the transition from an agrarian republic to an urban/industrial order in one giant leap, not gradually as in, say, the case of Switzerland. The Progressive Era rose up against the plutocracy, but that movement only expanded the Leviathan State even more: The direct election of U.S. Senators (big money controlling now those races) and the introduction of the income tax (rich folks take their money offshore, middle class folks gonna pay tax today). The new order transformed the Democratic Party from the Jeffersonian establishment of William J. Bryan to the big city socialism of Franklin D. Roosevelt. The New Deal, however, didn't work. By the late Thirties, unemployment was higher than it had been in 1932. Deficit spending and court packing schemes ignited a Southern Democrat-Western states Republican revolt from the heartland. By the late Thirties, FDR's vice president, John Nance Garner of Texas joined his fellow Texan, House Majority Leader Sam Rayburn to form an anti-big spending coalition to stave off future New Deal programs. It represented the last time conservatives ruled in Washington. The war saved the New Deal. In 1940, Democratic voters played it safe, choosing FDR over Garner's renegade challenge for the nomination. The GOP got nervous feet, too, nominating One-Worlder, Wendell Wilkie over America Firster, Robert Taft. That did it. The war turned into an ongoing social revolution. By 1964, not a single Southern Democrat attended that year's convention in Atlantic City. The GOP? The Republican Party of William Howard Taft, Warren Harding and

Calvin Coolidge was reasonable enough: Small government, tax cuts, industries protected, farmers prosperous, borders sealed, a nation at peace. America had that proper balance between the folk arts of small towns and those creative, industrious big cities. Nineteen-forty ended that Republican Party. In 1952, the Goppers chose Dwight D. Eisenhower over the more-seasoned Taft, causing Phyllis Schafly to bitterly lament that since 1932, every Republican Party presidential nominee had been chosen by the board of directors at Chase Manhattan Bank. By 1968, both parties had long taken Wall Street over Main Street: Industries unprotected, cheap labor flooding the borders, wages plummeting. A revolt boiled over, but both parties had left town.

THE BATTLES BEYOND

History, as the man said, never stands still. Life went on after the Grand Smash of 1968. So, too, did the South's glacial-like march to the GOP. That was sad, also. Back to Faulkner. You'd have to be from there. It was like folks were born with that Democratic Party donkey in the crib. No two words ever rolled off the tongue more naturally than "Southern Democrat." That was true before the war, the South being the party of Jefferson, Jackson, and Calhoun. It was more so after it. "Defeat made the South solid," Andrew Lytle liked to observe. It was a family thing. Folks agreed with the constitutional conservatism of Robert Byrd, Jr., Sam Ervin, and Richard Russell. And when they voted for those men, it was like pulling the lever for a grandpop, an uncle, a distant, but beloved kin. Even after the turmoil of The Sixties, folks would have preferred to stay in the Democratic Party. There was a class variable. Republicans were the Big Man in the office upstairs. Democrats were the fellows pushing the broom on the factory floor. Into the Seventies, the South remained Democratic at heart. But the national Dems sure didn't make it easy! The Dems, in fact, had long been a Massachusetts, New York, California thing. The party insisted on civil rights, but also on busing, affirmative action, abortion rights and later, the removal of the Confederate flag from public places. So without much enthusiasm, the South, from top to bottom, became Republican. My old senator, Jesse Helms, who worked as a press aide for Russell's abortive 1952 presidential run, was for a long time, a Dixiecrat in the Byrd-Talmadge-Ervin tradition. But that was an exception. Republicans were soon winning pretty much by default.

It was a different age. The Southern Democrat was no more. The "Southern Republican" never was. True, many Goppers had their roots in the Old South, but now they were members of The Party of Lincoln: Big business, yes; traditional values, let's not talk about it. Unlike Ol' Jess, they couldn't defend the region's history, even something as innocuous as saying nice things in public about Robert E. Lee, Stonewall Jackson, or Andrew Jackson. Men like Talmadge, Wallace, Ervin, Byrd, and Sam Rayburn would never come out against their homeland. Folks used to say, "if Sam Rayburn wasn't from the South, he'd be president" or "if Richard Russell wasn't from the South, he'd be president." A new world, indeed. Something was lost: Namely, a political party, that even as a defiant minority, stood up for the Southern people—-and the South—-as a distinct and living thing.

IX.

No Surrender

From my self-imposed exile, the traditionalist South looked pretty good in the American scheme of things. By the early Nineties, country music, commercial or not, seemed liked the only decent art form coming from the airwaves. In my youth, we all listened to the Opry on Saturday nights. In the mid-Seventies, that legendary venue moved from downtown Nashville to a theme park on the outskirts of town. The craftsmanship remained as sparkling as ever. Not just Nashville, but the creative life in Memphis, Austin, and New Orleans, not to mention the towns and hollows of Virginia and Kentucky, all prove conclusively that man lives by music alone; that is, he lives by poetry alone. In my time, the giants of the Southern Renaissance— Robert Penn Warren, Eudora Welty, Andrew Lytle, James Dickey, Walker Percy—were all going strong. In later decades, both Wendell Berry and Larry Brown, plus such Western North Carolina virtuosos as Fred Chappell and Robert Morgan all pumped life into this ongoing phenomenon. Music and literature. All preferable to politics! Unfortunately, democracy is the hand that's been dealt to you. In the spirit of Pat Buchanan and Sam Francis, one must play it. Into the Seventies and beyond, the South continued its losing battles against modernity. The roll calls are there, for all to see. Bill Cawthon, an independent scholar from Georgia, did the research. As history's losers, the South cannot receive a fair hearing. Recall the old adage used by Calvin Brown to describe the region's dilemma: Let's hang the son of a bitch and then give him a trial. In the culture wars, the South voted one way, the rest of America another. So permit a brief polemic.

- Immigration: Bowing to pressure from Asian diplomats, the U.S. Congress, in 1965, voted to open the nation's borders to non-Western immigration. Some debate that was. In the House, the bill passed, 318-95. In the Senate, it cruised by, 76-18. The Southern delegation voted no, 75-34. The rest of America (ROA) voted yes, 284-20. In the Senate, the South voted no, 15-10. ROA said yes, 61-3.

- School prayer. We're just getting started. In 1971, the House of Representatives debated a constitutional amendment to restore prayer in public schools. Needing a two-thirds vote to succeed, the measure failed, with 240-163 yes vote. The South voted yes, 84-23, well above the two-thirds threshold. ROA voted yes, 156-140, not nearly enough for two-thirds.

- Abortion. In 1983, with a pro-life president in the White House, there was another quixote attempt to amend the constitution, this time outlawing abortion. The Senate voted yes again, but well short of the needed two-thirds majority. The Southern delegation voted yes, 18-7, three votes short of the two-thirds. ROA voted 38-31, no.

- Women In Combat. Who said chivalry is dead? Eight years later, in 1991, the Senate sought to repeal a 1948 law prohibiting women from flying in combat missions. It failed by a wide margin, 69-30. The South voted yes, 15-10; that is, voting against women in combat. ROA voted 74-15 no, to go ahead with the motion and put those willing young ladies in the cockpit.

- Busing. By the mid-Seventies, desegregation had been achieved. Good enough? In 1976, the Senate took up legislation to bar Federal courts from hearing future busing cases. It failed, 62-29. The South voted no to such cases, 19-6. ROA voted yes, 56-10.

- Marriage. In the 2000s, numerous Southern states held referendums on the definition of marriage. A yes vote meant that marriage is defined solely as between a man and a woman. Do you have to guess the results?

- Texas: 76 percent, yes; 24 percent, no.

- Louisiana: 78 percent, yes; 22 percent, no.

- Mississippi: 86 percent, yes; 14 percent, no.

- Kentucky: 75 percent, yes; 25 percent, no.

- Georgia: 76 percent, yes; 24 percent, no.

- Oklahoma: 76 percent, yes; 24 percent, no.

- South Carolina: 78 percent, yes; 22 percent, no.

- Tennessee: 81 percent, yes; 19 percent, no.

- Alabama: 81 percent, yes; 19 percent, no.

- Arkansas: 75 percent, yes; 25 percent, no.

AMERICA ABOLISHED?

The Sixties are legendary for Great Society programs: Medicare, Medicaid, urban renewal, the National Endowment for the Arts, space exploration. Most dramatic of all was the before mentioned (several times now!) 1965 Immigration bill, the most significant legislation in American history, leading to changes so profound that no man can possibly bear them. As noted, the bill eliminated the National Origins Quota, one that confined immigration to those from the British Isles, something that came into being in 1924, as a response to public opposition to mass European immigration. The '65 bill was something new for the United States. As Mel Bradford once proclaimed, immigration, from America's beginnings onward, would be confined to those European nations. "Immigration from Asia and Africa," Bradford maintained, "was discouraged." Abolishing the quota was, as also noted, a Kennedy idea that went nowhere on the president's watch. After JFK's tragic end, however, the policy was resurrected. And so, an unforeseen (and unwelcome) expertise for me. No one cares. Why the hell should you? The transformation of the funky, low life of my adopted NYC circa 1975 to 1980 had plenty to do with it. So did the "Hey ho, Western Civ must go" hate speech on college campuses. Plus, there was all the doom and gloom on the Bob Grant Show and the more articulate arguments made in *Chronicles, National Review* and *The American Conservative,* mostly from the Old Right crowd I later ran with: Tom Fleming, Sam Francis, Chilton Williamson, Jr., Peter Brimelow and Scott McConnell, not to mention Pat Buchanan's jeremiads in *The New York Post.* From those pages to such tomes as Brimelow's *Alien Nation,* Chilton's *The Immigration Mystique* and Buchanan's *State Of Emergency* came a striking moral case against mass immigration. Americans, in short, never voted for the wide scale changes in the nation's population makeup.

Still, a loser issue. The Democrats needed the votes of the immigrant population. The GOP had to serve big donors who want that endless stream of cheap labor. (They are also scared stiff of the Hispanic vote.) Still significant. No man who grew up in the Sixties and Seventies can hold a particularly optimistic view of human nature or "the future." No man who grew up in those decades could recognize the nation that emerged in the Eighties, Nineties and beyond. Busing and immigration. Here are the two biggest wipeouts in modern American history. Where were you? If busing orders didn't affect your school district, if immigration didn't transform your town, city, county or state, well then, *O Lucky Man!* If so, another story. Back to the sad irons. Think of the tens of millions of Americans who can no longer recognize their hometowns, the streets they grew up on, the schools they attended, the landmarks of first dreams, first love. What social engineering did was create a tribe of exiles, a people without a voice, a political party, a nation and—the cruelest cut of all—a history: A people who would go the grave, the ravenous grave, mourning a lost world.

The culture war kicked off in the Sixties. In 1968, the U.S. Congress, bowing to pressure from the American Automobile Association (AAA), dumped the February 12 Lincoln holiday and more ominously, the once-revered February 22 Washington holiday. The latter's birthday was now a three-day weekend. In 1971, Richard Nixon did away with even that, bunching the two days into a meaningless "President's Day." After being in slumber for nearly two centuries, the Thomas Jefferson-Sally Hemmings hoax made a comeback being recycled again in the late 1990s as to protect Bill Clinton's weaknesses. And who can forget that 1969 episode of *Room 222*? A history class at this fictional Los Angeles high school held a poster contest concerning that subject. A balding, middle-aged man, a self-described "history buff" sat in. Two black students produced a Lincoln exhibit. Only it concentrated on Lincoln's racial views, portraying the Great Emancipator as a man who, in fact, would hold the whip hand over the freedman. The history buff stormed out of the classroom in a huff. *Et tu,* Abraham Lincoln?

The South took a stand. The region's opposition to the Second Reconstruction was measured and scholarly. George A. Shuford, an Asheville native who represented the area in Washington from 1953 to 1959, duly signed the 1957 "The Statement of Constitutional Principles," a learned document detailing the South's legal opposition to the *Brown vs. Board* opinion. Another native of Western North Carolina, Sam Ervin, the state's senior senator, was very much Horatio at the Bridge. Ervin was from nearby Burke County. He later gained national fame as the voice of the U.S. Senate during the Watergate hearings. He was also a strict constitutionalist and for that, a beloved figure in the state, never being contested for re-election. Ervin, in the mid-Sixties, was also co-chair of the Senate's Immigration Subcommittee. Along with Strom Thurmond, he did the heavy lifting against the '65 bill. Ervin's opposition represented the politics of self-preservation. He felt that the 1924 bill should be left intact since it was, after all, an Anglo-Saxon culture that gave America its language, its common law, its political philosophy. Plus, the '65 bill itself was discriminatory. It would favor immigrants from the Global South and was thus biased against the very same people who, as Ervin reiterated, founded the republic in the first place. Thurmond, too, stood on solid ground. He declared that there was nothing wrong with a people defending their cultural identity in the face of mass immigration. It all fell on deaf ears. By 1965, history had steamrolled both men. In the pre-Pearl Harbor America, cultural integrity, which can also mean cultural exclusion, was considered common sense, the desire of a people to preserve and nurture a 4,000-year-old civilization. After the war—and the shocking encounter with National Socialism—such thinking was obsolete if not fascist itself. In a post-colonial world, Anglo-Saxon was becoming code words for oppression. Anyone in the world, providing they adhere to certain cultural norms, can be an American. Anyone in the world can be British, Canadian, Australian or a New Zealander.

Facetious, you say? No, this is very much the conservative worldview, as articulated by none other than Ronald Reagan. Anglosphere values are universal. The liberal agenda, on the other hand, is calculating, cold-blooded, logical. Mass immigration is a blunt instrument to punch out those working-class and middle-class constituents that gave Nixon and Reagan their landslide victories. Finally, Ervin, it appears, gave American civilization too much credit. The U.S. had now become not just a welfare state, but a television nation. Most importantly, it was a suburban nation. Folks would soon live and work in the suburbs. They raised their children in good, suburban school districts. They worried about property taxes and college tuition. To oppose immigration would be racist. To their discredit, suburbanites didn't want to hear what Senator Sam was telling them.

And so, chunks of America, 100 years after Appomattox, look to have surrendered to mass immigration, legal and illegal, from Asia, Latin America, the Middle East and all points east, west, north, and south. That happy little nation of John F. Kennedy, Roger Staubach and Johnny Glenn now vanished forever. *Spurlos versenkt.* Sunk without a trace. A century after Appomattox, something else happened.

This time, the South didn't surrender.

X.

My Seventies

We kept traveling to Ohio. My mother missed the home place and we kids still loved the Seven Mile Inn. Austintown remained a Boys Town for my brother and myself, plenty of uncles to horse around with. Youngstown, on the other hand, was becoming a wasteland. You'd drive by the once-mighty Sheet & Tube mill and see nothing but emptiness, weeds growing around the rusting factories. Sheet & Tube became the story of Youngstown. In the Sixties, the city remained a manufacturing powerhouse. Once we drove through the bungalow belt on a late summer afternoon. We spied a middle-aged man snoozing away on a hammock. "Look at that man," my mother said sympathetically. "Resting after a l-o-o-o-n-g day at the mill." That was the best job these men would ever have. That was Youngstown, too, the City of Steel. Uncle Tony once told me that his hometown was the largest steel producer in all of America. Little Youngstown, I thought? No way! Back in Asheville, I talked with Marky's father about that. He was an executive with Asheville Steel, a modest plant in South Asheville. "What is the top steel city in America?" I asked. "Youngstown, Ohio!" he promptly replied, smiling. Youngstown! Number one! Not Pittsburgh, Detroit, Chicago, Gary, or Cleveland, but the town of Stiv Bators, George Shuba, Andy Kosco, Dave Dravecky, Ray Mancini, "Devo" and "Kool And The Gang." I felt a rush of ancestral pride.

Youngstown roared through the Twenties and even the Depression Thirties. In 1930, its population was 150,000 and the city was being planned for 200,000 residents. A moment of truth was reached in 1952. Sheet & Tube went on strike. President Truman was incensed. An armistice had been reached in Korea, but there were still hostilities, still a staggering amount of casualties. Sheet & Tube provided much of the muscle for the war effort. A strike, Truman was positive, would jeopardize the truce. And so, he tried to nationalize the plant and prevent a walk-out. The case went all the way to the Supreme Court, where the black-robed wizards decided that Truman had gone too far. The case, *Youngstown Sheet & Tube Company vs. Sawyer*, limited presidential powers in such matters. Was Youngstown in decline even then? The march to suburbia was on. By 1955, there were more Americans working in the bureaucracy than in manufacturing. Sheet & Tube took its knocks, as American jobs began hemorrhaging overseas. Then on Sept. 19, 1977, it happened. Five thousand workers reported to the job, only to be told they had been laid off. Fired. It was a genuinely tragic moment. Fellows walked back across that long bridge separating the plant from the parking lot. Several stopped halfway, took off their steel work boots and hard hats and just chucked them into the river below. Consider those millions of kids all across the Midwest: They weren't interested in college, they just wanted that hard hat job. Youngstown without Sheet & Tube was like New York without Wall Street or Rockefeller Center.

The city became a symbol of Rust Belt decline. Presidential candidates made the pilgrimage. Bruce Springsteen penned a ballad, "Youngstown," about a laid-off worker. A documentary, "Still Standing" was produced and released. The feds promised largess and certain construction projects, none of which materialized. Austintown was different. By the Sixties, its transformation from a rural small town to full-fledged suburbia was complete. The little village with the big Farmer's Market, the town that nourished both of my parents was gone. Still, The Lordstown Ford plant kept Austintown flourishing. Once, when Uncle Tony and myself were driving to Cleveland for an Indian game, we passed it. "They make 60 Fords an hour at that plant," Tony said admiringly. The Ford

Pinto was a Lordstown specialty. Its existence saved The Inn, giving it, year in and year out, a steady stream of lunchtime customers. For Youngstown, however, there looked to be no tomorrows. Forget 200,000. Its population was eventually less than Asheville's. The demise of the Rust Belt. Call it wipeout, number three. How'd it happen? How did America lose that one-paycheck supports all family? By going off the gold standard and seeing inflation rise? By Congress approving cost-of-living increases to Social Security benefits, forcing employers and employees both to fork over that much more in withholding taxes? Greedy corporations? Or demanding unions? Is that why manufacturing jobs went south? Cold War paranoia (countless nations telling America: If you don't give us free trade, we go to Moscow)? America opened its markets; others closed theirs to American goods. Think China, India, Brazil, Vietnam, Pakistan, Indonesia. What havens! No unions, little environmental regulations, no pensions, no health care plans, cheap labor by the *billions*. "Once, I made you rich enough," sang Springsteen in "Youngstown," "rich enough to forget my name."

In the Seventies, Asheville took a hit, too. Downtown, once the center of the county, was empty. It was sad, but all planned by the Money Boys. In 1966, a big mall was planned for East Asheville. However, folks didn't like the idea. They preferred life in that still funky, honky town downtown. Heeding the voters, the Asheville City Council ordered any construction on the mall to cease and desist. No matter. The Money Boys went over the heads of the council to the State Supreme Court, which promptly overruled the council vote. When the mall was constructed, the downtown establishment also headed east. Department stores, music stores, clothing stores, bookstores—-gone! The Farmer's Market was long gone. And worse. The Plaza Theatre—gone. The Imperial Theatre—the same. Now you took your dates to a cramped duplex at the local mall, instead of those majestic theatres with an upper balcony and classical architecture (a perfect place to watch *Gone With The Wind*).

Give Asheville credit. The city fathers knew young people were leaving. They made a public effort to stem the tide. It worked. A key moment came when Claude Ramsey, an Asheville patriot, located his

Akzona office building not on the outskirts of town, but right there in the middle of Pack Square. Instead of the mighty Vance monument being surrounded by boarded-up storefronts, derelicts and petty punks, it had a shiny tower and its office personnel to frequent other establishments. And there was more. In the late Seventies, the city fathers inaugurated a street fair, Belle Chere, as a way to attract folks downtown. This effort was imbedded greatly by the rise of Warren Haynes, a world-class guitarist for, among other bands, The Allman Brothers. Warren's family and mine were friends. His older brother, Tim, was a top star on our Little League teams and as was custom, his younger brothers, Brian and Warren were also chosen to play for us when their time came. Warren grew up on Pearson Drive (named for a once-famous diplomat) directly behind Weaver Park. His father, a quiet, kindly man, worked at a local supermarket. He was a single parent, like Fred McMurrary in *My Three Sons*. From the mound and at the plate, Tim powered us to many a victory. Brian and Warren eagerly played, but they had big shoes to fill. Brian, too, was a pitcher. On game day, no swimming was allowed (it got you too tired to play), but once, my father, the team's head coach, ordered us to go to the park and work out with Brian, to make sure he got his fast ball over the plate. We dutifully trudged to the park, but just lazed around all day. Why bust it out? Wait for the game. Brian was willing, but nervous. He had big shoes to fill. All the while, Warren was honing his craft. In the early Eighties, he started jamming at North Asheville's late, lamented main hang out, Caesar's Parlor. Soon, he was off to Nashville to play for David Allan Coe. Then to New York, where he became lead guitarist for The Allman's, who played regularly at The Beacon Theatre on the Upper West Side. He played in Phil Lesh's (of Grateful Dead fame) band and his own trio, Govt. Mule. Warren had now succeeded James Brown as the hardest-working man in the business and his stardom contributed greatly to Belle Chere's success. An Asheville patriot living in New York, Warren also played an annual Christmas concert at the Civic Center. The concert quickly became the hottest ticket in town. Asheville has a relatively small downtown, not difficult to rebuild. The abandoned Kress's department store became an apartment building. The S & W cafeteria with its Art Deco architecture (the symbol of downtown

Asheville) also reopened under new management. Whenever I went to a Vance High School reunion, I noticed that many of my former classmates were still living in town or elsewhere in Buncombe County. At a 1994 reunion, our old principal, Mr. Stanley, showed up. He commented on how great it was that so many of his old charges had returned to town to start and raise families. But not all of them did. Sometimes, you must leave a place in order to discover it.

My father, as readers may guess by now, was a go-getter. As a boy, he loved Saturdays (no school!). And, as he once told me, he always wanted to get up early on that magic day, so as to enjoy every minute of it. He loved life. On weekday nights, my father turned in early, never had insomnia and got up before dawn. On Saturday, we worked half the day in the yard, before enjoying sandwiches and sodas and a ballgame in the afternoon. Even on Sunday, my father couldn't stay still. He had to drive out to the warehouse, just to tinker around.

My father wanted us to stay on the ball. He would agree with Douglas Southall Freeman's famous dictum: Time is precious, waste it not. (His own calling might be: You've got talent, waste *that* not.) Whenever he caught me in a dreamy mood, acting lazy, he'd lay down the law. "What do you want to do with your life five years from now?" he'd ask. "Where do you want to be?"

Five years. Christ, Pop, that's a lifetime away. Who knows? He got the usual mumble, Ah dunno and that was that. Like any dreamer, I did have plans. My mind was on the big city, the sweet smell of the New York City subway stations, elegant brunettes, myself hard at work behind a typewriter. In high school, my claim to mere existence was baseball statistics: American League MVP in 1948, National League home run king in 1934, etc. It kept those simple-minded suckers entertained on the bus ride back to North Asheville. My ball playing days were over, couldn't make the adjustment from Little League (45 ft. from the pitcher's mound to home plate) to Babe Ruth League (now Big League markers, 60 ft. to the dish). But I still loved the game, its intricacies, its endless talent for surprise, the ambience of the ballpark. There was *The Asheville Citizen* of Richard Morris and Larry Pope, two fine scribes, plus all the sportswriting greats mentioned in Chapter IV. There was the book I read in the ninth grade at the downtown library. It was about sports writing. All the fellows enjoyed getting together at the big winter baseball writer's banquet in New York for drinks and horseplay. (In the mid-Thirties at the height of his fame, Tom Wolfe was invited to that year's bash. According to biographers, the novelist just sat in awe, staring at Ruth, Gehrig, Ty Cobb, and Jimmy Foxx enjoying drinks and cigars.) There was *The Odd Couple*, with Oscar, the carefree sportswriter on the prowl in the big city. The life! I duly joined the student newspaper staff at VHS and later, did the usual intern drudgery at *The Citizen*.

Along the way, however, I found, as noted, something better. The year? 1975. A Periclean Age? No, but not a Dark Age, either. 1975, add 'em up: *JR* by William Gaddis, *Humboldt's Gift* by Saul Bellow, *The Fight* by Norman Mailer, *A Month Of Sundays* by John Updike, *Pages From A Cold Island* by Frederick Exley, *Memoirs And Opinion* by Allen Tate, *Democracy and Literature* by Robert Penn Warren. My tastes were boringly conventional. I only knew what I read about in *Time, Newsweek, The New York Times Book Review* and *Saturday Review*. Still, it was a fun time. I wasn't in college and my pals and I could enjoy books and talking about them without having to put up with professors carrying on about "theory" in, say, the poetry of Emily Dickinson. (Only recall that kick-ass scene from the short-lived late Seventies television series, *Skag*, where Karl Malden played a Pittsburgh steelworker. One of Skag's sons wants to be a dentist, the other is drifting, working with his pop at the mill. In arguing over the future, the millworker tells his girlfriend, "I don't need to go to college to have some professor tell me how good Faulkner is. I *love* Faulkner.")

I had run away to Manhattan. A job (dishwashing again!), a room at the Y, a Royal typewriter. We Manhattan boys read books by the bushelful. We enjoyed books. I had pitched tent at the 23rd St. YMCA and discovered a Manhattan isle awash with A-1 bookstores on every other street corner. We talked about books, including the detective paperbacks by Dorothy Uhnak and John Gregory Dunne. We talked about novelists, especially the 1979 *New York Times* magazine cover story essay by John Gardner, with the author blasting away at contemporary novelists for their "tinny" moral view of potentially catastrophic times. "You gotta love the way these intellectuals battle each other in public," my friend, Steve Miller, a prematurely balding native New Yorker and like me, a would-be aesthetic, laughed. It was funny. All these writers—-Gardner, Barth, Bellow, Updike—had made it in the Great American Game of dough, success, and fame. Look at them squabbling amongst themselves! Books mattered. Authors mattered. Their moral vision mattered. For any aspiring writer, this proved a hard task ahead.

Steve and Gary Wazowski and myself did all this while washing dishes, delivering groceries, clearing off tables, working as doormen and shipping clerks, while paying the rent, keeping the clothes washed and dried, the belly full. We read foreigners, too: Joyce, Dostoyevsky, Tolstoy. But I liked American authors better. With Bellow and Richard Price, there was the immediacy of city life, its struggles, chaos, chances for redemption. With Updike, Cheever and Joseph Heller's *Something Happened*, there was the middle class tale, a place where the journey from avarice to morality was also paramount. Later on, the world of Wendell Berry and the arts of husbandry, one that suggested, too, an outline of sanity; plus, finally, Larry Brown, the fireman-turned-author who sang of the working class, small town Southern folk that we middle class kids brushed elbows with on a daily basis.

What did these giants have in common? They captured, to me, the urgency, the madness—and the occasional sanity—of mid-to-late-twentieth century life. There was the world where abundance, cynicism and honest struggle all existed side-by-side. With Wendell Berry, the way home: The road to the self-sufficient, prudent, careful, responsible world of the American Founders. Again, this came into focus decades later.

The mid-to-late Seventies was a fun time. I can remember exactly where I was when I first read Kerouac's *Desolation Angels*, Wolfe's two masterpieces, *Look Homeward, Angel* and *You Can't Go Home*

Again, plus Faulkner's *The Sound And The Fury*. Even the light detective novels were fun. Those scruffling years in bookstore-laden NYC represented my prep school for college.

CHAIN REACTIONS

Reading amounted to a chain reaction, one author to another, one genre to a different one, one worldview to the next. Fiction reading led to fiction writing. No soap there (it's something you're born with). Nonfiction reading led to nonfiction attempts. Thanks to the years of failed fiction writing, this was a little easier. And on that score, more chain reactions: *Firing Line* to *National Review*, the 1985 40th anniversary issue and the short bios of the publication's earlier greats: James Burnham, Russell Kirk, and Richard M. Weaver. *NR*, too, meant Old Right warhorses Chilton Williamson, Jr., and Joseph Sobran. In those more ecumenical days, *NR* also meant ads for *Southern Partisan* and *Chronicles*, which led to the world of Tom Fleming, Sam Francis, Murray Rothbard and especially, the great Bradford. (*The New York Post*, meanwhile, meant Pat Buchanan, the only one of these authors known to the public.) The Old Right directed me to the Vanderbilt Agrarians and especially again, to Donald Davidson and Andrew Lytle. So, what is an author (as the French deconstructionists might term it)? Youth and glory? It gives way to the Lytle-Davidson world view. Writing not for glory, but to keep something alive. In short, the writer as a bard, as a poet for his people. The Fugitive-Agrarians saw the South as a fighting cause, a healthy remnant of Lytle's unforgettable phrase, "a republic of families." And more. "This is ours," Lytle proclaimed in the masterpiece essay "The Hind Tit" from *I'll Take My Stand*. "And if we have to spit in the water bucket to keep it, we'd better do so." Yeah, I can remember exactly where I was when I digested those lines (living room, one-bedroom apartment, Little Neck, Queens, Friday evening, sometime 1990). Who can say no to such a cause? It was home, yes, the South, but also a resistance to modernity that made sense to me (see voting patterns, Chapter IX). A Christian civilization, one that demands, above all, self-denial, is a sure road to adulthood, to the world of responsibility and commitment, the only world that keeps civilization from crashing through the thin ice it always skates upon.

The cause of the South is the cause of a republic: The world that Bradford, Wilson, Francis, and Buchanan championed in column after column, essay after essay, book after book. At first, it seemed doable. The Old Right of the late Eighties and early Nineties was alive, full of energy. It gave conservatives an alternative to business-as-usual: Opposition to mass immigration, to free trade with underdeveloped countries and especially, to the 1991 Gulf War. The Old Right worldview was liberating. Let's not, on one hand, "control" spending, but just eightysix the whole apparatus (eliminate a good 500 Federal programs, for beginners). But let's, on the other, protect jobs (come back, Sheet & Tube!), protect, too, the border (come back, pre-1965 America!), while staying out of unnecessary wars (come back, pre-Pearl Harbor America!). This isn't to mention an unyielding stand for traditional values (come back, the 10th amendment). In fact, let's just bring back that Golden Era of the Grover Cleveland-Theodore Roosevelt-William Howard Taft-Warren Harding-Calvin Coolidge America, where folks were too busy raising their children and revering the past to save a fallen world.

Again, as much as you want to, you can't avoid politics. The Old Right peaked in the Nineties, first with Buchanan's challenge to George H.W. Bush in the 1992 presidential primaries, followed by his culture war stemwinder at that year's convention all the way to the 1996 primaries, where Buchanan, with the eyes of the world upon him, did win the New Hampshire primary before falling victim to the greatest smear campaign ever inflicted on an American presidential candidate.

Life was elsewhere, with the Euroskeptic parties of Europe: The National Front of France, The Northern League of Italy, The Swiss People's Party, The Danish People's Party, The Sweden Democrats and The Freedom Party of Austria, all delivering an opposition to immigration and multiculturalism, abortion and gay marriage and, in general, to a tyrannical European Union rule, a movement that at least party-wise, is entirely lacking in the United States.

My search for the West had a Sixties connection, ironic, but truthful. We were children of the Cold War. The West is free, the East languished in chains. Eastern Europe, to me, was a dark place: Cold, gray, a land where the sun never shone. There was the U.S.—U.S.S.R. ideological showdown. At the same time, there was a Western Europe and North America convulsed in full-scale social revolution: The world of liberation, drugs, legalized abortion, no-fault divorce, nihilism in general and soon, low birth-rates. Eastern Europe, as my friend Paul Gottfried shrewdly observed, was immune to all this. The Iron Curtain, as Paul maintained, served as an unintended protective coating from the barbarism of the West. And as Phillip Roth added: Eastern Europe was a place where nothing goes and everything matters, while the West was disintegrating into a joint where everything goes and nothing matters. In the late 1980s, Baltic nations and neighboring Russia celebrated 800 years of Christianity. To me, that was amazing. You couldn't imagine the United States celebrating 800 years of anything. Since the fall of the Berlin Wall, Eastern Europe and Russia have managed, for the most part, to stave off Western decadence. Such nations seek to maintain a Western, Christian civilization, exemplified by tax credits for young mothers to increase fertility along with the spine to say "no" to abortion on demand, gay marriage, and the great migrant invasion of Europe. Who knows? Maybe there is a remnant, after all.

The world of reading and writing and the world of Asheville went hand-in-hand. One comparison is Oxford, Mississippi and its patron saint, William Faulkner. This, too, represents the world of bookstores: Asheville with Malaprop's and The Captain's Bookshelf as independent bookstore gathering places and Oxford with Square Books on the location made famous in the closing scene of *The Sound And The Fury*. For me, the Asheville connection was Wolfe on one end and Weaver on the other, a cast of thousands in between. Wolfe: The prose poet of romantic youth, reading, reading, then writing, writing, writing. Youth as fame and love. "I wrote 10,000 words today," the man would chant while storming the Brooklyn Bridge for late-night walks. Weaver: A more somber side. A quest for the meaning of community, the very meaning of civilization. A quest for a world where people know each other, feel related to each other, share the same morals, manners, and codes of conduct. Don't worry, plenty of individualism, too! "Personality is that little private area of selfhood in which the person is at once conscious of his relationship to the transcendental and the living community," he wrote in *Ideas Have Consequences*, articulating his social bond individualism thesis. Yes, man, somehow, needs to find the road back to living by poetry alone. In Asheville, it seemed doable. The old (and new) Pack Library, the World's Greatest Newsstand, *The Sporting News* at Lord's Drug Store, Malaprop's, Captain's Bookshelf and especially, The Book Trading Post on Market Street downtown. In the early Eighties, there was no better place to be. Fifty thousand titles, you say? And countless of them for a buck each. Two Golden Ages of American Lit came together: The modernists of the Twenties and the Thirties and the postwar boom era of the American novel, traditionalists like Bellow, Updike, and Walker Percy alongside such postmodernists as Pynchon and Barthelme. One day, I promised to read Mailer's *Of A Fire On The Moon* in one sitting. And I almost did, until the clerk told me, correctly, to buy that thing or else get the heck out.

Those modest venues—and the jewels within—set me on a journey into, first, the world of possibilities and in time, my own struggle for the survival of the West. And it could have only started in an Oxford, a Manhattan isle chock full of bookstores and, of course, an Asheville. So God bless the hometown of the great Grover Cleveland, but I sure am glad that job didn't open up for my father in snowy, old Buffalo.

Coda:

IF HEAVEN DON'T LOOK

"I have got used to being a foreigner everywhere, and it would fatigue me to be expected to be anything else," so claimed the young T.S. Eliot. At first an exile, yes; a foreigner, no. Then, in time, that too. Life in exile has its benefits. Keeps you on your toes. As it turned out, Asheville stayed on my mind, more than I had imagined it would. My adopted hometown had changed too much. On one hand, it got much too expensive. In the late Seventies, I could stay at a room at the West 23rd Street Y for $31 a week. By the millennium, an apartment the size of a janitor's closest would cost up to $1 million. In 1995, I had my ducks lined up. Published and with an agent who shared my conservatism, I could march into Manhattan from bucolic Mineola with that volume on Richard M. Weaver under my arm and feel that New York might yet be a city for conquest. Alas, I was way too naive to think that any New York publisher, even a non-ideological one, would do a book on Patrick J. Buchanan, even though my subject was, and is, a household word. Maybe down the road.

The outer boroughs, meanwhile, were no longer Archie Bunker/ Tony Manero country. My adopted New York was now populated with strange signs, languages, faces. There's a life in exile for you.

As late as the Eighties, I still believed Asheville would remain mostly the same, save a mini-mall here and there. Into the Nineties, this was no longer the case. The town did rebound handsomely from the recessionary Seventies and soon word went out that this mountain town not, say, super-expensive New York or San Francisco, was the place to be. According to Fred Chappell, "Keep Asheville weird" had become a rallying cry once the new carpetbaggers took root. What to do? Write about it, write it all out. In fact, I had a ball. What a town! In Asheville, all roads led to big Zeb, the longhaired country boy who remains the most popular politician the Tar Heel state has ever produced. It was a straightforward history, no frills, part narrative, part sketches of the city's notables. There were the pols, just not Zeb Vance, but also Richmond Pearson, the quiet, effective diplomat and Reynolds, the colorful America Firster and immigration restrictionist. The Civil War brought not only Vance, Coxe and McDowell, but Zeb's 26th Company, 43 of which marched out of Asheville on May 3, 1861, with only one man making it back home alive. There was also room for the teachers: Doc Gullickson, the prolific classicist, an architect of UNC-A's Western civ curriculum, plus the basketball coaches/mentors of my youth: Ted Carter and C.L. Moore. And of course, the jocks: Charlie Justice, Henry Logan, and Mary Montgomery, the 1972 Olympiad who is *never* mentioned in the other histories of the mountain town. Most of the jocks were stock car boys that I too remembered from my youth: Banjo Matthews, Dean Dalton, Harry Gant and later on, Robert Pressley. The creative Asheville list not only included Wolfe and Weaver, but also John Ehle, Gail Godwin, Wilma Dykeman, Michael McFee, Jonathan Williams and outside of Buncombe County: Fred Chappell, Robert Morgan, and Jim Wayne Miller (if a writer made it to the cover of *Time* or *Newsweek*, I felt beholden to see what all the publicity was about. Same was true of authors who grew up on the same streets, same town, same area as you did). There was a celebrity or two (Rev. Billy Graham and Warren Haynes), plus the newspaper boys that once greeted me every morning: Bob Terrell, Richard Morris, and John Parris (an anonymous reader said I was guilty of hero worship).

Happy endings? When did the Southland ever have one? A conservative people. A liberal nation. How is that possible? In June 2020, barbarism, at last, prevailed: Monuments and statues of men once revered in America—Christopher Columbus, George Washington, Thomas Jefferson, Andrew Jackson, John C. Calhoun, Robert E. Lee, Stonewall Jackson, Jefferson Davis, Jeb Stuart, Theodore Roosevelt—vandalized, torn down, melted, destroyed. Little Asheville was not spared. The great Zeb lost his monument in Pack Square! A public school for the man was renamed. A monument for Buncombe County's Civil War dead removed. It happened. It didn't happen. It can't be so. No one's going to run me out of Asheville. Pack Square? Hail—and farewell!

Back to Mary M. Here is a good way to end our tale of family life from the solid side of The Sixties. Mary's family, as I remember them, was typical of the boom era: she had three female siblings and an older brother, Wesley. Her mother coached the Asheville YMCA swim team. Mary's older sisters, striking brunettes, also swam, but Mrs. Montgomery found a record-breaker with her youngest daughter. Mary's father, Wayne, served as Asheville's mayor, successfully navigating the city through the tense times of the late Sixties. Mary was the star of the Y team, lapping her opponents in meet after meet, winning medal after medal. (I played a (very) minor role on the Y team, filling out as a backstroker on a medley relay team.) Mary's teammates all knew she was fast-tracked for the 1972 Summer Olympic squad, which she did qualify for. This was a big deal, not just making the squad, but doing so as a girl from the snowy Western Carolina mountains, a town that enjoys the four seasons when all the other girls were from California or Florida, states where they have sunny, swimming weather year-round. In Munich, Mary swam in the individual medley. Her race was in the afternoon, stateside-time and would be replayed that evening on Asheville's ABC affiliate. That afternoon, I sat in Spanish, last class of the day, looking forward to Mary taking home the gold in the delayed broadcast. Suddenly, the teacher, Mr. Chandler, blurted out, "Oh, by the way, Mary came in sixth in her race." Wha-a-a-t! Sixth? No way! Even worse, I knew the result, spoiling the evening for me. "Why'd you *say* that?" I shouted back, a shy boy who never spoke in class. "Don't *say* that!" I became theatric, throwing my arms up in disgust, burying my head on the desk. Chandler was taken back, but only slightly so. "Okay," he waved me off. "Just pretend I never said it." Chandler laughed. The idiots around me all roared. I suffered in solitude. Didn't these dummies know that I swam on the same Y team as this Olympiad, traveling to Spartanburg, Greenville, Kingsport, Tennessee, representing the Land Of The Sky? Didn't they see how important that race was to me? I dutifully watched the broadcast, glumly anticipating the result.

Back home, they had a ceremony at the Vance High auditorium. Students of all grades filed in, glad to be out of class. Mary's friend, Jane Victorino, recited a poem of appreciation. The refrain, as I recall, was "sixth in the world," as in "To be sixth in the world...," praising Mary's persistence in going from the far-flung mountains to Olympic glory. Mary stood by, shy. These were only high schoolers. Maybe they should have hailed her as "the Olympiad" instead. The ceremony came and went. In the meantime, Mary went back to competitive swimming, winning the North Carolina Female Amateur Athlete of The Year four times, the last one in 1975, when her career ended. The Montgomery's were a large family in a North Asheville neighborhood chock full of selfless middle-class folks. Her parents were civic-minded, dedicated to the upbuilding of modest Asheville, just like my old man, driving around town, looking for an ice cream shop with a lineup of Little Leaguers, all jammed packed into a white, '64 Volkswagen bug.

So, a fun book. And a tribute. It was also a welcome break from the decline of the West doom and gloom tomes that would occupy past and future efforts. What I didn't do was ask friends and family back home the usual: Ah, I'm doing research, what's it like these days? I knew the responses.

"Son, I'm telling you, it's changed so much, you wouldn't recognize it!"

"These foreigners are pouring into Asheville!"

"You know what they call it? 'San Francisco in the mountains.' The city council had to pass a law keeping panhandlers off the streets!" (Images of Haight-Asbury 1967 now running through the brain.)

One summer, I purchased a fine photo/history paperback on McCormick Field. The historic ball yard, renovation completed, was packing them in, so much so that there was talk of accommodating the burgeoning fan base by building a new field by the French Broad River.

And so, I didn't ask. On vacations home I'd let friends and family pontificate as they pleased. My adopted town was unrecognizable. Didn't need more of the same. What of it? Life in exile has its charms. Teach us to care and not to care, as Eliot pleaded. And so: 9 a.m., Saturday, clearing Mrs. Shibley's lawn full of debris; 8 a.m., Sunday, digging into those big pots at Grace; 4 p.m., weekdays, football practices until dusk, knocking helmets with the Randolph Street fellows; and 5 p.m., Saturday, the Merrimon-Midland bus finally arriving at the Square, the passenger settling back into those big, cushiony seats for the safe ride home. "If heaven ain't a lot like Dixie," sang Hank Junior, "I don't want to go." Yes, and if it doesn't look like Asheville, circa 1962, I might just want to take a pass myself.

Latest Releases & Best Sellers

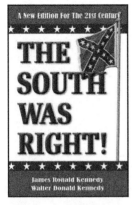

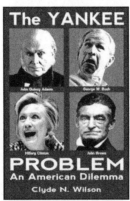

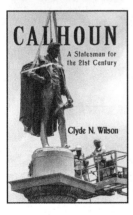
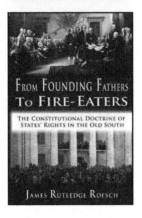
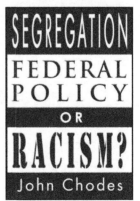

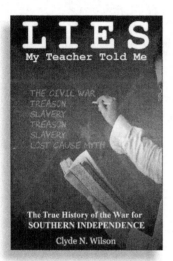

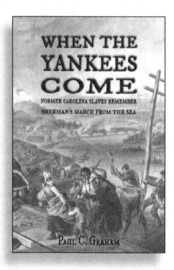

Printed in Great Britain
by Amazon